WINNING THE
BATTLE WITHIN

DR. GLEN ALBAUGH
MICHAEL BOWKER

Kele
PUBLISHING

Notice
Mention of specific companies, organizations, or authorities in this book does not
imply endorsements by the publisher, nor does mention of specific companies,
organizations, or authorities in this book imply that they endorse the book.

KELE PUBLISHING
164 Por La Mar Circle
Santa Barbara, CA 93103

For information regarding special discounts for bulk purchases, please contact Kele
Publishing Special Sales at 1-530-622-3532 or Kelepublishing.com

Manufactured in the United States of America

10 9 8 7 6 5 4 3 2 1

The Library of Congress Cataloging-in-Publication Data is available
Glen Albaugh
    Winning the Battle Within/ Glen Albaugh—Rev. ed.;1st Kele Publishing ed.
    p. cm.
    1. Golf—Sports – United States 2. Golf – Mental game – United States.
I. Title
    DNLM: 1. Golf – inner game – Popular Works. 2. Sports – peak per-
formance – Popular Works. 3. Mental preparation for sports – new concepts –
Popular Works. 4. Improving your golf game – Popular Works
TXu1-213-199
ISBN 978-0-9762931-2-5

*To my Father, Reuben Albaugh, a life
long source of inspiration, and to my Mother,
Vira Albaugh, who believed I could leap tall
buildings in a single bound.*

CONTENTS

ACKNOWLEDGMENTS

During the past four decades, I've been lucky to meet some incredibly talented and insightful coaches, athletes, sport psychologists and teachers. We've shared experiences and ideas, discussed new theories, and tested old ones. We've played and coached and laughed and argued and debated and sometimes we shared a good bottle of wine or two until well after midnight. These are my great friends and colleagues and to them I owe a tremendous debt of gratitude. For it is truly their wisdom that laid the foundation for, *Winning the Battle Within*.

The book found its magic when Michael Bowker, my coauthor, agreed to help me condense decades of coaching and sport psychology experiences into graceful and compelling prose. Thank you, Mike, for the countless, stimulating, discussions, and for your steadfast guidance and eternal optimism.

To my boyhood friend, Michael Murphy, whose insights into the inner game are full of imagination, humor, and great truths. Michael, who, of course, is the author of *Golf in the Kingdom*, generously shared his unique vision of the game, and inspired me to write *Winning the Battle Within*.

To Scott McCarron, one of golf's true gentlemen. Since 1993, Scott and I have completed more than 30 *Winning-the-Battle-Within* workshops together. Over the past decade, we've worn out cellular phones talking about the game. Scott's articulate explanations of many of the training tips — as well as his overall insights from the professional level — are invaluable to this book. Most of all, Scott, thank you for your enduring friendship.

To Pete Carroll, one of America's dynamic and elite coaches. Pete knows the inner game as well as anyone in the coaching profession today. Thanks, Pete, for our long friendship and for leading me to a greater understanding of the value of contingency practice.

To Bill Walsh, my friend and coaching guru. Words like 'respect' and 'admiration' don't seem big enough somehow when you were talking about The Coach. His friendship and counsel were driving forces toward the completion of this book and it is dedicated to the memory of all the incredible things he brought to my life and to this book.

To Kirk Triplett, whose capacity to learn is enormous, and for sharing your knowledge of how professionals practice, and your willingness to do old things in new ways.

To those who have long supported me at the University of the Pacific, especially Sport Sciences Department Chairman, Tom Stubbs. To the Pacific administration, who always gave me the latitude I needed to teach the inner game, and to test my theories in live settings with fellow coaches, professors, athletes, and students.

To the pioneering professional golfers who took chances on my start-up career. Thank you to Jerry Foltz, Brad Bell, Steve Haskins, John Kennady, Brandon Goethals, Bobby Siravo, Dana Dormann, Jenny Park-Choi, and Brian Tucker.

To Aaron Bengoechea and Tyler Williamson, thank you for being with me from the start.

To John Flannery, my treasured friend and first professional client, who bragged about me on national television and jump-started my work on the mental aspects of sport.

To the talented Pacific golfers, who for 20 years contributed profoundly to the evolution of the material that went into this book.

To the brilliant and innovative Pacific Sport Sciences graduate students who acted as sounding boards for my developing theories, including: Beth Brown-Duran, Kristy Schroeder, Pete Schroeder, Karin McConnell, Ted Leland, Linda McDonald, Karla Konet, Bucky Layland, Julie Hickey-Holt, Mark French, Mary Eberhardt-Sandstrom, Bryan Collier, Mike Westafer, Cindy Spiro, Roger Brautigan, and Patricia Dyer.

To Kevin Sverduk and Kris Baxter for their commitment to *Winning the Battle Within* and willingness to spread the principles among their students.

To Eric Jones and Hilton Tudhope for reading every word and offering valuable editing advice.

To my lifelong friends, Charlie Reynolds, Larry Mitchell, Phil Kelly, Lee Megginson, Bill Ayer, and Jim Carlstrom, who participated in early *Winning-the-Battle-Within* experiments with great enthusiasm. Whether we were in San Jose, Incline Village, or Fall River, we learned together to trust our swings.

To Taras Liskeyvich and John Dunning, and the other fabulously talented coaches at Pacific, with whom I spent countless hours discussing all phases of the coaching process that appear in many chapters of the book.

To Tom Quinn, with whom I've debated the virtues of teaching technique and WBW concepts for three decades.

To Douglas Eikermann, whose eagle-eye made this book shine. Mike was right — you are world-class.

To my golf friends in northern California: Phillip Herrera, Steve Simpkin, Bill Corbett, Kirk Kashevaroff, Tony McBroom, Rod Souza, Steve Wolfe, Jeff Tokunaga, Bob Olds, Earl Stewart,

Dick Dalligiacoma, Jim Ono, Bucky Jackson, Bill Giffen, Jim Nylen, and David Florsheim.

To Nick Ushijima, whose mastery of the inner game has allowed him to be successful around the world, at whatever he does.

To Jeff Brehaut, Charlie Wi and Roger Tambellini whose persistence and willingness to change are extraordinary, and who belong on golf's greatest stage. And to these great, young, players who will all win their fair share of tournaments in the future: Philip Dawson, Robert Hamilton, James Watt, John Ellis, Brian Dillon, Andy Moren, Matt Hansen, Jason Higton, Han Lee, Zoran Zorkic, Ricky Barnes, Andy Barnes, Spencer Levin, Ashley Gomes, Dana Arnold-Ebster, and Anna Temple. And to the next wave of aspiring professional golfers — Dillon Dougherty, Ryan Thornberry, Reid Scarf and Marc Peterson.

To Ty Caplin, my first swing coach, friend, and collaborator. Ty opened the door to the fabulous Northern California Professional Golfers Association, which has been so supportive of our *Winning-the-Battle-Within* workshops.

To my friends — Laird Small, Tommy Masters, Eric Pollard, Kris Moe, Gus Jones, Mike Mattingly, Steven Frye, and Jim Toal — great golfers and teachers, all.

To the enlightened coaches — Teri Greene, Ria Quiazon, Anne Walker, Nancy McDaniel, Val Verhunce, and Cy Williams.

To the future stars — Ashley Noda, Lauren Salazar, Christopher Petefish, Belen Hernandez, Andrew Bonner, Daniel Covrig, Jessica Thielamay and Kyle Bowser for their early commitment to WBW.

To the "sensuous sportsman" Larry Meredith, for showing me that the spiritual journey and the sport experience are not mutually exclusive.

To my special European friends, Sean Corte-Real and Herbert Forster, for their commitments to *Winning-the-Battle-Within* principles and for challenging me to explore further the inner corridors of performance.

To Jennifer McCarron, who returned to her first career in time to serve as an energetic editor for this book.

To Barb Paris and Diana-Alberts Kimbrough for faithfully making my yellow pad scribbles come alive on the computer screen.

And especially to Sandy Albaugh, for starting and presiding over Albaugh Enterprises, and most of all, for reminding me to dance as if no one were watching.

— GLEN ALBAUGH
Stockton, California
April 30, 2009

INTRODUCTIONS

From the late and greatly missed BILL WALSH, member of the National Football Hall of Fame, and winner of three Super Bowls as coach of the San Francisco 49ers.

I guarantee that if you apply what Glen has to say in this book, you will become a better player. During our long-time friendship and our many professional collaborations, Glen has maintained a passionate commitment to the improvement of sports performance.

I was happy when Glen told me he was preparing this book. It was gratifying to see that my longtime friend was going to finally put his vast knowledge of what goes on; what should go on; and what shouldn't go on—in between the ears—down on paper. I was also delighted to play a part in the process.

This book is a real treasure for those who love to play golf. Not only will you come away with new and refreshingly new strategies for practicing and then taking your game to the course, you will make an extraordinary leap in your enjoyment of the game. By learning how you can choose to be confident, how to remain in control of your game through positive self-talk, and how to master your fears, this book can lead you directly to the winner's circle.

I highly recommend you read this book not once, but several times because Glen's teachings have remarkable depth. Many of his techniques have long been utilized by top performers throughout the world of sports—including my 49er teams. *Winning the Battle Within* represents a major advancement in our understanding of what it takes to achieve peak athletic performance.

From SCOTT McCARRON, PGA TOUR Player

What are your goals when it comes to golf? Better yet, what are your dreams? What do you deeply enjoy about the game? What kind of golf do you long to play? As you think about your answers to these questions, do you immediately think of your swing mechanics? Probably not.

Golf is not about the perfect technical swing. It is so much more. And that is why this book about golf is so important. Dr. Glen Albaugh shares the methods he has developed and taught to me—and many other players of all calibers for decades. It is an invaluable reference for amateurs and professionals alike.

What were my goals and dreams? Getting my PGA TOUR card. Winning on the PGA TOUR. Making a living doing what I love to do. I can honestly say that I have reached them because of my work with Dr. Albaugh. And with his help, I am constantly striving toward new goals. You can, too. You already have it within you.

From PETE CARROLL, head coach of the University of Southern California Trojan football team, winner of the 2003 and 2004 NCAA National Championships. Pete is also the former head coach of the New England Patriot football team.

Glen Albaugh has long been my teacher and friend. His teachings helped form the foundation of my coaching philosophy. Every athlete has something to learn from Glen. He combines a wealth of knowledge about sports, golf in particular, with an integrated vision steeped in Eastern thought and the Human Potential Movement. The result is a riveting set of lessons, mental strategies and hands-on practice drills that combine to prepare golfers to achieve peak performance.

For more than three decades, Glen has maintained an unwavering commitment to coaching and teaching. Now, in cooperation with a variety of players—from champions like Scott McCarron and Kirk Triplett, to players who dream of breaking one hundred—he presents a cutting-edge approach to the game that is unparalleled in its wisdom and practicality. I especially like his approach to practice, which mirrors the newest thinking of top coaches in football and many other sports, and guarantees golfers more efficient and consistent performance. This is a good book. It should be in every golfer's library.

From MICHAEL MURPHY, author

My longtime friend, Glen Albaugh, is a leading facilitator of *The Kingdom's* lessons for learning and performing golf skills. Within his special relationships with golfers of all abilities, including top professionals, Glen has developed practice regimens and a mental game process that will help anybody's game.

By combining Eastern thought with sport psychology and motor-learning research Glen is making major contributions to quality simulated practice strategies that fully activate kinesthetic imagination. I'm proud to say that we have collaborated on a number of projects including training workshops, cooperative symposiums, and work with Russian sports psychologists. Glen is a passionate, forward-thinking professional.

You will find that this book offers a wonderful alternative to swing mechanics or equipment technology for playing more consistently and learning to enjoy the game.

From MICHAEL BOWKER
April 5, 2009
Santa Barbara, California

I am excited to be working on this book with Dr. Glen Albaugh because what he presents in these pages will help you play better golf and have more fun doing it. For those of you who don't know Glen's background, he is an applied sports psychologist and longtime sport psychology professor and golf coach at the University of Pacific in Stockton, California. He works with nearly fifty pros on various tours, including Scott McCarron and Kirk Triplett, as well as hundreds of amateurs of all skill levels. Along with being one of the nicest guys I've ever met, Glen has an almost mystical understanding of the game and those who play it. By that I don't mean mystical in a hot-tubby, cultish sort of way. What Glen teaches is grounded and it works.

For example, he says things like:

You can choose to be confident
The perfect swing is the one you trust
You must let go of your swing to gain control
What you see and feel in your imagination, you can do
Always ask yourself, "What did I learn? What am I
    doing right?"

Glen's experience with athletes is far-reaching. At Salinas High School in Salinas, California, he and boyhood friend, Michael Murphy, started the school's first golf team in 1947. If they saved their summer money, they could play Pebble Beach Golf Links for $5 per day. Murphy would later found the Esalen Institute, a center for the Human Potential Movement, in Big Sur, California, and write what is still considered the most transcendent golf book of all time—*Golf in the Kingdom.* (If you haven't read it, or Murphy's sequel, *The Kingdom of Shivas Irons,* you owe it to yourself to pick up some copies. There are wonderful messages inside.)

Glen was a good athlete. He was a tough, rebounding forward at Hartnell College in Salinas and San Jose State before graduating. He started his coaching career at Washington High School in Fremont, California, in the San Francisco Bay Area. His teams won league championships and he formed a fast friendship with the school's young football coach, Bill Walsh. Later, of course, Walsh would gain legendary status for winning three Super Bowls and inventing the 'West Coast Offense' as the coach of the San Francisco 49ers.

Bill and Glen have enjoyed a lifelong friendship. They spent hundreds of hours together sharing coaching philosophies and at Bill's invitation, Glen extensively observed the 49er's at practice during their Super Bowl years. Bill was a great believer in Glen's teachings.

"Our discussions are always rewarding," Walsh said. "Glen's work on the mental processes athletes can use reach peak performance is something we used at the 49er' camps. Every athlete can benefit from what Glen has to say."

Glen also served a stint in the United States Army and coached at Santa Rosa Junior College, California State University at Hayward, and the University of Utah. He completed his doctorate, with a sports psychology emphasis, at the University of Utah.

During those years, Glen was attracted to the Human Potential Movement, which was becoming popular among progressive thinkers. He was especially intrigued by the concepts of self-acceptance, self-determination and development and the successful integration of all the components of our personality—the physical, emotional, intellectual and spiritual.

"The idea that we can make the choices that allow us to control our own lives really appealed to me," said Glen. "There is an almost unlimited power inside all of us, if we only know how to reach it. I also became very intrigued with the concept of transferring this self-determination into the realm of sports—particularly golf."

In 1971, Glen joined the staff at UOP where he was a professor in sport sciences teaching sport psychology and coaching education. He also coached the men's golf team for more than two decades. One of Glen's protégé's is Pete Carroll, coach of the two-time national champion University of Southern California football team. Carroll credits Glen as being an important source of the concepts that he has used to understand, motivate and psychologically strengthen his great teams.

"I've always considered Glen a mentor," Carroll said. "His concepts helped me form my own philosophies about coaching, sports and life in general. I still talk to him all the time. I certainly wouldn't be where I am today without Glen."

Much of what Glen talks about in this book has application far beyond the golf course. I've read most of the golf books on the market, and I found what Glen has to say completely refreshing and new. His ideas have lead hundreds of players to a completely new mindset about golf, and in many respects, life itself.

1

HOW THE PROS
AND TOP TEACHERS
ARE USING THIS BOOK

We are excited to present to you this second edition of *Winning the Battle Within*. With the first edition being sold out — thanks to golf enthusiasts in the U.S., Europe and Japan 'getting it' when it comes to the critical importance of the inner game — we thought you might enjoy these additional first two chapters, which were not part of the first edition.

If you are like us, your friends and loved ones have, on more than one occasion, rolled their eyes and declared how we love to play golf; and what they say is true, but what only golfers know is that we also sometimes fear the game, sometimes even hate it as it humbles and ridicules us with seemingly no remorse; and sometimes we love, hate, fear and love it again — all in the day and in the same round! This is not something you can should try to explain to someone who does not play the game, nor should you try least that person comes to believe that you have totally flipped your lid, and of course, that person would be right when it comes to those of us who love the game.

1

Since the book was originally released, we've received reactions to the lessons embedded in *Winning the Battle Within* from dozens of the best players and coaches in the world, and each has a unique insights. Their comments were fascinating and some, like Scott McCarron, Charlie Wi and Kirk Triplett, attribute a significant part of their success on golf's highest competitive platform — the PGA Tour — to the concepts in this book. Others, including USC football coach, Pete Carroll, are using them in arenas other than the golf course. We thought we would share some of these insights and comments with you in a new and exclusive chapter, followed by a second new chapter that captures how Coach Carroll, one of the most successful collegiate coaches in America, has made the WBW concepts the centerpiece of his tremendously successful coaching philosophy. What follows is a close look at how, in their own words, these premier players and coaches are using *Winning the Battle Within* on the practice tee and the course. We think these new chapters offer a terrific 'opening hole' that can definitely lead you to higher performance levels and more fun on the course.

SCOTT McCARRON: Poco a' poco!

One of the most intriguing stories came from Scott, who talked about facing one of the most pressurized moments in his highly successful PGA playing career — fighting to keep his playing card his rookie year.

"It was 1995 and I needed to finish alone in third place or higher in the last tournament of the year, the Las Vegas Invitational, to keep my card," said Scott. "Everything was on the line going into that tournament and I really felt like I needed Glen there to keep me in the right frame of mind. If I had to return to 'Q' School, there were no guarantees. I felt that I might be playing for my career."

Shortly before the tournament, Glen's father and lifelong mentor, Reuben Albaugh, passed away. Reuben's memorial fell on the same weekend as the Las Vegas tournament and Glen could not be there to work with Scott.

"I knew Scott had to shoot well that weekend, but after the Friday round, he seemed pretty far back," remembered Glen. "Then on Saturday he came roaring up the leader board with a fantastic 64 to move into 6th place. I knew if he played well on Sunday, he could move high enough to keep his card. It was exciting news."

Sunday morning Scott called Glen and asked if he had any thoughts or words that could help him face the enormous pressure that would present itself the next day.

"That Sunday was an unusual day and my thoughts were centered on my father's life, his writings, his friends, our family, and his experiences," said Glen. "From these thoughts emerged a wonderful quote that my father used. He attributed it to one of his great friends, Julius Trescony, with whom my father collaborated on many university-sponsored agricultural field projects. The two of them also often hunted mule deer together in the rugged Ruby Mountains in Nevada. The saying that my father loved, and that I gave to Scott that morning was 'poco a' poco se andan lejos', which colloquially translated means, 'Never hurry in the mountains' or 'little by little we travel far'.

"I was looking for something from Glen and what he told me was perfect for the situation," said Scott. "All day on Sunday I repeated the phrase to myself before every shot. 'Poco a' poco' was such a resolute thought that I found a calmness come over me that I'd never felt before. I stayed in the moment all day and I did not hurry once."

Glen recalled, "After the funeral we sang Dad's favorite songs and read his poetry and told stories of his life. There was a special energy in that church that day and I wondered afterwards whether

Scott felt it somewhere deep inside. When I returned to Stockton that night, I clicked on the Golf Channel. I hadn't even sat down yet when Scott's picture flashed on the screen and the commentator said that 'Rookie Scott McCarron finished in sole possession of third place today with a brilliant 65'. I didn't even have time to shout out in celebration because the phone rang and it was Scott.

"'Poco a' poco se andan lejos'!" said Scott. "Your Dad was with me on every hole and especially down the stretch. I was calm and confident all day."

Concluded Glen, "Because Scott had diligently prepared his mind for performance and practiced developing a creative imagination, he allowed something great to happen that day. His remarkable play was not a miracle or a product of chance. It was the product of choice, made possible through quality practice and playing in the imaginative mind."

"It's a lesson that's never left me," said Scott. "The teachings in *Winning the Battle Within* permeate every part of my life, not just golf. I always work to stay in the positive, not dwelling on the negative. I stay in the moment while playing with my children, and I utilize everything from positive self talk to visualizing success throughout my day, regardless of what I'm doing. It is how I live my life."

CHARLIE WI: Self-Belief is the Key

Two days after giving this interview Charlie nearly won the Honda Classic in Florida. He was praised by the commentators, including the iconoclast himself, Johnny Miller, as being a player who is "definitely gaining confidence." It was an opportune comment because Charlie had just been talking to us about how Glen's teachings were helping him choose to be confident. "Self-belief is the key to success on the PGA Tour and at all levels of golf," Charlie,

37, who hails from Thousand Oaks, California, told us. "Glen helps me believe in my game and he's helped me get out of my own way in that I believed there was a 'perfect golf swing' out there and I needed to find it. Now I know that the perfect swing really is the one you trust. You are always going to feel insecure on the golf course. Even when you play your best golf insecurities set in all the time. It's all about how you deal with it. It's not that your heart isn't beating fast and you aren't feeling like choking because everyone is, it's how you can use Glen's tools to move that aside and concentrate on the positive — the images of a successful shot.

"As a rookie, I had a self-image issue. When you start worrying about what others think of you, you don't perform your best. Glen's concepts helped me realize that nobody out there is even freaking thinking about me! It's only about me and how I handle the pressure, using the routines, on the course and the practice tee that he lays out in this book. One of those concepts that I've really come to embrace is goal-setting. I wasn't as serious about that at first, but I've come to realize it is critical in visualizing what kind of player you can become. My ultimate goal is to become a major championship winner. It's about self-belief in the end."

LAIRD SMALL: 'Transfer Training' at Pebble Beach

As Director of the Pebble Beach Golf Academy, Laird is one of the nation's leading instructors in the art of 'transfer training'. Laird was the PGA national teacher of the year in 2003. Nearly everyone who has ever spent time on the practice tee can appreciate the concept — transferring the skills we learn and hone on the practice tee to the course. It's one of the most difficult and often frustrating elements in golf — but one of the most critical. How many times have we heard (or muttered ourselves) "Man, I was hitting it so well on the range, but now that I'm on the course I can't do anything!"

"Bridging that gap is one of the most neglected parts of teaching," said Laird. "Glen's ideas are perfectly formed to help make that transfer. The SAT process, the contingency practice on the range, and the introspection skills he teaches are ideal for building that bridge from the practice range to the course."

Laird has been instrumental in helping players focus on making this transfer. Sometimes it works so well he gets an unexpected response from his students. "I shared some of the concepts in this book with a student, who was also a friend of mine, and I could see on the range he really 'got' the process. He went out and shot the best round of his life. He came back in and asked, 'Hey, what is this stuff you are teaching? I can't touch it or see it, but it just made me a way better player. I think its voodoo golf! I love it!'

"What he was experiencing was playing in his imagination," said Laird. "He was able to take what he was doing on the range and doing it equally well or better or the course. There is a big vacuum out there right now in terms of transfer training because it is hard to teach and it takes time, but it's really at the heart of playing better golf. I'm most effective as a teacher when I can help build awareness within players and Glen's tools really help me do that.

"I often ask my students to pay attention to the next golf telecast they watch, especially when the camera gets in tight to the players and you can hear them talking to their caddies. After the club selection is made, the conversation almost always ends with the caddy or the player repeating a phrase, like 'trust your swing' or 'just let it go' or some other key that helps them move away from the mechanical world into the world of feel and imagination. Witnessing that helps my students realize there is another entire element to playing better golf.

"When I teach, I always allot time for the inner game. I use all the drills and at the end of my lessons, I give a copy of *Winning the Battle Within* to my students and say 'read it!' Their instruction isn't complete until they do."

TERI STRATTON-GREENE: Ladies Love WBW Too!

Teri is the highly successful head coach of the women's golf team at the CSU Monterey Bay in Seaside, California. Her team was ranked 19th coming into the St. Edward's Invitational at the Gray Rock Golf Club in Austin, Texas this spring. Just prior to the tournament, the team spent a "wonderful day with Glen and Laird Small, at the Bayonet Golf Course in Monterey," said Teri. "It was the first mental coaching my team had received. When we arrived in Austin the next day for the tournament, the wind was blowing about 30 miles per hour. But, it was if the team didn't even notice the wind. They walked tall, no stories were told and they didn't complain, even though all the scores were high. They played with trust and confidence. They told me after the tournament that they just tried to stay present at all times. On the second day we shot the lowest score of the tournament. We ended up surprising a lot of people, but not ourselves, by finishing third in the tournament. We came away from that experience a much better and trusting team."

KRISTY SCHROEDER: These are Lessons for Life

"The principles from *Winning the Battle Within* that have helped me the most include the concepts that focus on what I can control," said Kristy, the highly respected former head coach of the UC Santa Barbara softball team. Kristy now lives in northern California and works as a WBW consultant at Pacific. "Whether I'm playing a sport, or involved in other aspects of my life, when I focus on the things that I can control, I accomplish much more. I think self-talk and staying present are also key concepts for me. If things aren't going well, I'm able to turn them around with positive self-talk, a positive attitude and the walk of the Matador. Last, but certainly not least for me, suspending judgment is critical. That's the concept that I've struggled with the most. If I can just describe what my behavior is, and then suspend judgment, I'm much more effective in whatever I do. I use these principles in my everyday life, whether it's raising my children, meeting new people, coaching, teaching, or consulting. They are the foundation of my personal and professional philosophies. I think the concepts that Glen touches upon in his book can be transferred into all walks of my life. My husband, Pete Schroeder, is a professor at Pacific and sport psychology consultant, and I discuss it with him on a regular basis. It's a must-read for everyone."

ROGER TAMBELLINI: Taking Suspension of Judgment to a New Level

Yet another young and tremendously talented player, Roger has won twice on the Nationwide Tour and he's headed for a return to the Big Show this year. He's worked with Glen since 2000 and says that the teachings in the book provide new ways to remind players of old principles.

"I take away different ways to do what you have to do," he said. "For example, the whole notion of taking one shot at a time, Glen will tell me seven different ways to do that. He puts things in ways you can use. One of the key things for me is being patient, but Glen added a critical element. He talks about the game actually starting when you are driving carefully and patiently on the way to the course. One of my problems has been that I speed through my life, my round and my shots. He told me to be mindful of being patient, even when I'm brushing my teeth in the morning before a round. Be patient and be in the moment. I also now write down all my goals and I love all the drills, especially feeling the swing when I have my eyes closed. It's amazing how feeling my release through impact is magnified with my eyes closed.

"This year I feel I made a breakthrough by taking suspending judgment to a new level. I used to hold things inside and not show emotion and I thought that was suspension of judgment, but last year I really did move past every shot once it was struck. When you play winning golf, you aren't thinking about anything except maybe a simple swing feel, like tempo or rhythm. Judging yourself doesn't even enter your mind."

ERIC JONES: Booming Drives and the 'Aha!' Teaching Moments

Eric can hit the ball a far distance. How far? Well, he was the Remax World Long Drive Champion in 2003 and has smacked more than a few drives over 400 yards without hitting the cart path. That's far! Today, Eric still plays competitively and teaches at the Pleasanton Golf Center in the San Francisco Bay Area.

Performing in long drive competitions, as well as playing in regular professional regional tournaments, can generate some serious pressure. Eric attributes his ability to stay confident and trusting to many of the teachings in this book.

"Without a doubt, the information in these pages has helped me both personally and professionally in a profoundly positive way," he said. "As a player, it's helped me keep a better perspective on my game and my life, which has helped me improve the way I think, feel, and act. My game has improved, and I understand how to keep all parts of my life in better balance.

"Professionally, it's helped me learn to listen to the way my students think, feel, and act. That makes it easier for me to help them turn ifs, can'ts, and don'ts into when's, can's, and do's. Helping students better manage their emotional landscape is also easier. Their lows aren't so low and they can sustain their highs longer.

"The affect of this book on my internal and external confidence, and that of my students', is quite insightful. I know that my confidence has improved because I learned how to fall back on the hours of practice I put in. At the same time, I am better able to help my students put together practice plans that are more targeted to the skills needed to improve their play on the course. They tell me they are able to act with a level of confidence they did not have before.

"Hitting the ball long and playing well overall, requires trust and commitment. When a student finally 'gets' the concepts of trust and commitment, it is like a sudden 'Aha!' moment for them and their game changes significantly, and most often, permanently, for the better.

In addition to conducting a unique, on-course teaching program, Eric has written some excellent e-books on what it takes to hit the ball longer and straighter. You can check out what Eric offers at: Ejones@targetcenteredgolf.com.

MATT HANSON: Making the Cut with His Eyes Closed!

In one of the most amazing stories we heard from a player or coach, Matt talked about learning the ultimate form of trust from Glen and the WBW concepts. Here is Matt's eye-opening — or closing — story.

"I have used a number of Glen's concepts and drills throughout my career. One in particular, stands out. Glen and I had been working on the release of my putter. He had me putting with my eyes closed on the practice green, which helped me exaggerate the feel of my release. During one round on the Nationwide Tour last year, I had been struggling to duplicate the nice release that I felt on the practice green. I hadn't made a putt all day. With only a few holes left on Friday, I realized that I needed to make a birdie coming in to make the cut. But on the next hole, I was faced with a three-footer just to make a par and the pressure was really on. I shut my eyes and felt that nice release and made the putt.

"The dramatic moment, though, was on the 18th hole. I had a ten-footer for the birdie, and had to make it to play on the weekend. I so fully trusted Glen, and was so confident that I could achieve a good release, I committed to closing my eyes and putting the ball. I released the putter, stroked it with trust, and the ball rolled right into the center of the cup! I don't putt with my eyes closed on all putts in competition, but by using the eyes closed drill in practice I'm consistently reminded of the importance of a tension free release.

"Glen's teaching has helped me so much to trust my game and commit to great strategies. I wouldn't be at the level I am at today without Glen's help."

MARC PETERSON: Drilling for Gold

A young player with immense potential, Marc fully trusts the drills and concepts in the book to help him in his career on the Canadian Tour and beyond. "Last year I had only a few shots that I could rely on," he said. "It's my goal this year to be able to work the ball whenever it's necessary. That's why the nine-ball challenge drill is one of my favorites. To execute that drill you have to be completely aware of your golf swing. If it heads in the wrong direction, you have the feel and understanding through your post-shot routine to correct it sooner. I also use the inner game (trust) drills and this year I'll be working hard on my SAT score. Suspending judgment is also key to moving on from a missed shot or high-scoring round. I constantly learn from Glen and these principles. I think one of the most valuable tools I gain from him and this book is the reminder of what I previously learned. Much of this is basic, but it is so easy to get away from it. This keeps me focused and trusting of my swing whenever I encounter periods of tension."

NICK USHIJIMA: Making a 100 Percent Commitment to Every Shot

"Using what Glen teaches, I've developed a system that works for me, based on playing to my strengths and making a 100 percent commitment to every shot," said Nick, the CEO of Susquehanna Corp., an international real estate investment company. Nick played for Glen at Pacific and went on to win more than 40 tournaments in the U.S. and Japan, including the 2000 and 2007 Japan Mid-Amateur and the 2000 San Francisco City Amateur Championship. "I analyze my game based on what I do best. Although I am not a long hitter, I am very straight. My wedge, short game and putting are my strongest points. I now base all my strategies around those advantages.

"No matter what the situation, I do not hit a shot without 100 percent commitment, which means I don't select a shot that I have less than a 90 percent chance of pulling off. If I get into trouble, I often don't take any risk getting out, but rely on my short game to save a score. For example, I have a system whereby I don't even try to hit a shot over a hazard, or obstacles that penalize heavily, unless I have a 4 iron or less in my hand. I analyze all shots with this 'probability assessment'. It is all part of Glen's teachings to play to our strengths.

"Learning about your own game is so much a part of *Winning the Battle Within*. I am conservative in most things I do in business, and in life in general, so I try to keep it that way on the golf course. In other words, I never do something 'not like me'. This helps me commit to everything I do on the course. Knowing one's realistic ability and capability is important. Over the years, Glen taught me how to realize this and how to incorporate it into building my game."

TOMMY MASTERS: The Art of Teaching Others to Trust

Besides having one of the great golfing names of all time, Tommy is one of the premiere teachers in Northern California. He's helped PGA Tour sensation, Nick Watney, and many others, learn to further trust their games.

"Glen made it clear that trust is something that is a feel-oriented message and that every golfer has to create that feel and trust deep inside. He injected in my brain that when you work with a player, you must be able to give them the information they need to trust their swings and their entire game. You can be a technically adept teacher, but if you can't also teach players how to trust, you will be limited in what you can do for them. That's what the concepts in *Winning the Battle Within* do for me; they give me the tools to help my players build trust inside themselves."

Tommy, who has twenty years of teaching experience, played on the Canadian and Nike tours. He is the Director of Instruction at San Joaquin Country Club in Fresno California. He works with Watney, Marc Peterson and other budding stars and so far, an amazing 25 of his high school students have gone on to play NCAA golf.

HERBERT FORSTER: 'Confidence is a Choice!'

A former player on the Pacific golf team, and now one of the foremost instructors in Europe, Herbert recently 'came out of retirement' to play an intense competition, with national pride at stake. He prepared by going back to Glen's teachings for strength and calmness. He emailed us his story of the match.

"'This is it!... I can feel it again!' Herbert began. "After several years of not playing competitively and focusing much more on the coaching side of the game, I suddenly could feel it again: Pressure, adrenaline, hopes, fear and uncertainty.

"It was the Portuguese Team Championship in 2007 (held in a Ryder Cup-type format) and friends, like Portuguese national amateur champion, Sean Corte-Real, had talked me into participating, and supporting their team. We made it into the finals, and I was the last man out, with all other matches finished and a tied team score....Last hole, last shot into the green with a 7 iron, whereas my playing partner only had a sand wedge in.

"'Now, I have a choice!' I told myself. 'Let the doubt, my missing tournament preparation, the nervous crowd, my hopeful teammates, the TV camera, etc., get to me and cause me to tighten and eventually choke; or to consciously trust my imagination, see and feel the target and let my swing happen naturally.'

"I swore to myself that whatever the outcome might be, I would enjoy that moment. I grabbed my club, confirmed my commitment to my strategy, aim and trust in my pre-shot routine, and stepped into the shot. Even before I started my swing I knew I had it and stroked it perfectly. The ball hit the flag stick; I won the match and the overall championship with the team.

"Not winning, but the feeling of deep trust and inner peace on this 18th fairway are what still touch me when I think about that day. Once again I realized that this is what *Winning the Battle Within* is all about, and it contains everything we want to pass on to our students in a nutshell:

Accepting that we have the choice to be confident or not.

Getting connected to the target with all our senses.

Letting the imagination (sub-conscious) do the work.

Having appropriate means to practice all this.

"With the WBW drills and training techniques, we can offer

players, of all levels, a powerful hands-on approach to learn how to truly connect to the target, and how to let go of conscious control. Once we have accomplished this, we truly have won the battle within and we have the opportunity to reach our unlimited potential."

Herbert conducts *Winning the Battle Within* workshops in Munich, has his own version of The First Tee program there and consults with the German National Boy's golf team.

SEAN CORTE REAL: WBW Leads him to the Winner's Circle

Despite not playing competitively often over the past few years, Sean won the Portuguese Mid-Amateur National Championship this spring by a whopping 10 strokes. Although Portugal is his native country, Sean played for Pacific while Glen was working with the team, and now teaches WBW in Portugal. Sean credits WBW for his ability to reach high levels of performance, despite his lack of playing time.

"My goal in the event was to have the right strategy and stick with it," he said. "I managed to do that and focus on my routine, trust my swing and not worrying about what anyone else was shooting. It is amazing to me that after all these years with WBW and Glen, I am still learning and discovering new ways to do old things. I make sure to set goals for every round and every practice. It's almost like the next shot will be the last one I take. I absolutely love it, and enjoy every moment preparing for it."

Sean also told an amazing story of helping a struggling player rise to the occasion in the Portugal six-man team national club championship. The player, Antonio Castelo, was hooking the ball into trouble consistently and had been doing so for months. Sean's team needed Castelo to play well and Sean worked with him on the range. "I said 'Why don't you try hitting a few with your eyes closed to feel the clubhead'?" said Sean. "He hit the ball great that way. Then he opened his eyes and started hitting the 250-yard snap again. I suggested he play the entire round the next day with his eyes closed and he did! He shot his best round in ten years. This is a true story.

"I have taken WBW into my life and I try to live my life like I play golf, one shot at a time, one routine at a time; combined with a good strategy and total commitment to the plan and the shot."

DR. KEVIN SVERDUK: 'What is Your Trust Score?'

A 10-handicapper, Kevin, has a Ph.D. in sports psychology and teaches at Argosy University in southern California and California State University at Long Beach. Unlike McCarron, Triplett and most of the others in this chapter, he plays like we do — with resolve, determination and with a skill level that is more creative than stable. A former tennis professional, he has found the portal to golf is similar to his philosophies in tennis. "In both sports, you have to separate yourself from the external results and stay immersed in internal thinking; in the sensation of trust and focusing on the things you can control."

Kevin worked with Glen for several years at UOP, where he coached the university tennis team and now is a WBW consultant in Southern California. "Much of what we've talked about over the years is here in this book, and it is second nature to me now," he said. "Yet, with golf, it is a daily challenge to apply what I already know. That's what makes Glen's method of teaching so effective; the processes he offers constantly underscore how to implement these concepts on the course. What I find so valuable is that this approach is about helping people discover self-knowledge. It gives responsibility to the students and that is enormously empowering for them."

Kevin provides keen insight into the importance of focusing on the process, and not the outcomes. "It's a big challenge because the social environment is such that everyone always asks, 'What did you shoot? How many birdies did you make? The real questions should be, 'What was your Trust Score for the day? And, what did you discover about yourself as a person and as a golfer?' The day we get into the habit of asking ourselves those questions after every round is the day we can open new possibilities for ourselves on the course and in our lives."

KRIS BAXTER: Making the Game Fun Again

Like it does for a lot of us, golf stopped being fun for Kris after he completed his collegiate playing career at Pacific. Trying to make the Big Show became a psychological Purgatory, and he ultimately married, coached golf for a time at Pacific, and started Blagency, Inc., a highly-successful business promotional and branding company. He also teaches WBW principles golf near his home in Dana Point, California.

As he neared age 50, Kris began to look at his clubs, now gathering dust in the closet. He began to wonder, and he re-read *Winning the Battle Within*, and then began long talks with Glen. Inspired that he could follow Glen's processes, he began practicing and playing regularly. Then a funny thing happened. "I started having fun again, like I did when I was a kid," said Kris. "I no longer put such untold pressure on myself. I followed all of Glen's techniques and found I was caught up in the process and the outcomes took care of themselves. I gained a lot of confidence practicing my pre-shot routine, playing the course ahead of time on the practice tee, and I stopped all story-telling. What I noticed was that my friends who play — most of them were 10-to-20 handicappers, began picking this up from me. They all improved almost immediately and I saw externally how these processes could help every player."

Using the WBW golf techniques, Kris's game flourished to a point that he has taken dead aim at the Champion's Tour. "I'm playing much better than I did even in my college days," he said. "What's terrific is that I am learning something new about myself and my game every day. One of the things that made me stop playing was that I had lost the sheer joy of playing. When I picked it up again at age 49, I didn't expect it to be so much fun. But, it is! When I follow these techniques, I get caught up in the process and it is enjoyable on a deeply satisfying level."

TOPPER OWEN: This Feels a Lot Like Love

"Once upon a time, shanks, skulls, scoops, chili-dips, double-hit yips, and a dreadful seriousness descended on me like a plague of locusts," Topper, one of the top senior amateur players in California, told us. "In spite of these afflictions, I endured my golf, but it was not much fun.

"Fortunately, I heard the call for one of Glen's WBW workshops near my home in Santa Barbara, California. There were lots of ideas and drills; we covered an amazing amount of material. Still, I was struggling. I was afraid I was too far gone to be rescued by more instruction on the mechanics of the game. I needed something that got to the core of my troubles.

"During some short game exercises I expressed my thoughts to Glen. He diagnosed me as being in a negative emotional landscape, for which he prescribed positive self-talk. He also urged me to activate my imagination to create more desirable experiences in my golf game. I grabbed that life preserver and began the changes that really have transformed by golf game. I began to tell myself repeatedly that I had a trustworthy swing with a silky, sex-wax tempo. I imagined myself as well-dressed, disciplined and dignified as a matador. I began to identify myself as a golfer who could play extraordinary golf, who was quickly resilient after any negative experience, who was fiercely determined to become that version of myself, who could play like magic, who was truthful in present awareness, and at his best when trusting and tension-free. I repeated a mantra-like affirmation: 'I can do (this shot, this round, this game)...' Little by little, I began to achieve presence, an awareness of feeling, a focus on the task at hand, an anticipatory awareness of the sights, sounds, and feels regarding the shots before me during each round.

"Using Glen's techniques, I began to think of golf as fiction writing about oneself and the upcoming shots that could turn out to be true. Glen's wisdom is that we create our experience by how we imagine ourselves, our shots and our futures. It is a script written in the heart and mind, worked into form by practice, and then enacted on the golf course.

"After a time of working on the lessons in WBW, I entered the Silicon Valley Senior Amateur in the San Francisco Bay Area. Comforted and focused by this 'can-do' self talk and empowered by staying in the imaginative mind, I won the tournament. It was a big surprise, even though I had been telling myself all through the event that my task was simply to imagine whatever I liked, which included that I was, for example, playing the 9th hole of the first round and on my way to the winning score. Who was to say, at that moment, that the image was not true! We would have to wait and see, but in the meantime, it made for a pleasant moment on that 9th hole and seems inarguably to have helped manifest the outcome. I had come a long way.

"I am profoundly grateful to Glen. Golf has again become an enjoyable adventure, a medium for sharpening awareness and perception, an array of challenges that evolve us as players and people, a test of skill and an opportunity for honor, and providing special times shared with others. *Winning the Battle Within* is a path to a joy that ranges from the sensational to the spiritual. It feels a lot like love."

CY WILLIAMS: UC Davis Team Soars on Glen's Lessons

"Glen has worked with our team, here at the University of California at Davis, at different times, imparting the materials in this book to our players," Cy said. "Most everything we do as a team, in practice, reflects in some way, the ideas and philosophies that Glen has imparted on me. We are competing and hitting shots, wedges, and putts at every practice just like we would do so in a tournament.   This I've learned from Glen.

"We reached the number one ranking in the nation for Division II in April of 2002, and this year, in only our second year of competing at the Division I level, we have been ranked in the top 25 in the country for almost the entire season. We've done this without a single junior All-American golfer on our roster, which goes to show how powerful his methods are for helping players develop as athletes. There's no doubt in my mind we would not be able to accomplish most of what we've done without implementing Glen's philosophy into our program. His teachings are a must for anyone looking to improve his or her performance on the golf course."

SCOTT PUAILOA: "Why Are You Here Today?"

For Scott, the long-time Director of Golf at the beautiful and exclusive Valley Club of Montecito, California, the inner game now consumes about 90 percent of his teaching time. "I spend only about 10 percent on swing mechanics," said the personable pro, who once played for Glen at Pacific. "I teach my players most of the WBW golf drills, including tension-free, eyes closed, keeping the target in the mind's eye and the nine-ball challenge drill. I want them to develop internal feel rather than react to external feedback coming from me.

"The part of the WBW concepts that really intrigues me is playing in the imaginative mind. That's how I grew up playing in Santa Barbara. Then I fell into the golf culture's obsession with mechanics and I lost the ability to play imaginatively for a time. If you think about all the other sports, (Scott was a point guard and quarterback in high school and played free safety at UOP as well as being a standout on the golf team), you don't have time to think — you just react and play automatically.

"I teach a lot of CEOs and other successful people at our club and many of them already practice these techniques in their work. But they tend to fall into the golf culture's mechanical trap, and I use these drills to get them back into the imaginative mind. Nine out of ten people I teach are helped right away by the tension-free drills.

"Perhaps the most difficult thing for players to get through in a golf round is learning to suspend self-judgment. I always ask them 'Why are you here today?' You need to ask and answer that question before every round. If you haven't done that, fear can creep in and it's easy to start judging yourself because you aren't reaching your goals. That's usually going to be the case, if your goals are vague. Negative thoughts will always be there during every round, but if you know why you are there — what you are going to accomplish that day — you can deal with them.

"In any given round, I may be working on different parts of my mental game. But part of my answer to the question of why I am golfing today, is always: 'I'm here to win the battle within'. With this book, Glen just made it a whole lot easier to win that battle."

2

USC COACH PETE CARROLL ON WBW

One the foremost proponents of the WBW concepts is Pete Carroll, Head Football Coach for the University of Southern California Trojans. At a sports seminar in the winter of 2009, at Lakeside GC in Burbank, California, Pete was asked about the influence of the inner-game concepts of *Winning the Battle Within* on his phenomenal and on-going success at USC. Here are some of the responding comments from the future Hall of Fame Coach.

'A FANTASTIC COMPILATION'

"A long time ago, Dr. Albaugh started putting his thoughts in motion by testing them out on the students at the University of Pacific, about competition, performance, focus, discipline, and practice," said Pete. "Years later he was able to put all of these thoughts together in this book. I knew it was going to be good because I knew where all of this was coming from, and my feeling turned out to be accurate. He has created a great, eye-opening process for players and coaches and stepped into realms a lot of people haven't dealt with in terms of preparation, pre-and-post performance routines, and many other areas.

"In this book, he draws attention to the multiplicity of ways people can practice this game, and work at developing their skills. It's a fantastic compilation and I think he's way out there with it. I think with so much information in the world of golf, tactics and tools and aspects of the trade, this is one that's really going to make a difference for people and it's going to take them much deeper into their game, as they go about the process of making themselves better players.

CARSON PALMER AND SELF-TALK

"A clear example of a player who has benefitted from WBW, occurred my first year at USC. We had just finished a spring practice scrimmage and I was standing in line with quarterback Carson Palmer, who ended up being the number one pick in the NFL draft the next year. I asked him, 'How'd you do today?' He said 'Ah, like always, big scrimmage, I throw two interceptions. I haven't thrown two all spring and then I throw two in the big game.' I was flabbergasted by his language. I said 'What? You're saying that this always happens and it happened again and you're accepting it? I don't want you to ever talk like that again; you can never say that again, you can never hold that thought, that phrase. From this point forward, we're talking about what you can do, not what you did before. We're not having the kinds of conversation that can bring you back to an old level of performance and expectation.'

"We started shaping Carson's language, his self-talk. We worked on the way he addressed himself and how he related his experiences. We worked on getting him into a more positive, uplifting and constructive mentality. We started re-defining his way of looking at the world in terms of his athleticism and performance. I think his old ways would have continued to bring him down and keep him from becoming the player that he has become. That's an illustration of the power of self-talk. It is a huge factor in perform-ance and we need to pay attention to it.

THE TREMENDOUS POWER OF THE MIND

"There's a whole lot of learning to take place in this book. What's really exciting about it, for those who go for it, is players will find pathways into their psyche that they never really knew existed. There's a tremendous power we own as individuals that we don't tap because we don't know how to get at it. This book opens door-ways and approaches that people will not only score with on the course; they'll take it off the course as well.

"As we grow, we evolve. Yet, even as we evolve in physical ways, through strength training, conditioning, nutrition and all of the things that can give us more power and flexibility, this evolution will only go as far as a player's mind will take them. As important as physical condition is, the mental side of the game is even more powerful. All of the physical skill in the world won't help you if you can't perform well, and you won't perform well unless you can clearly allow yourself to do so. That's why all of these teachings and this entire process is absolutely instrumental to high performance — regardless of your size, shape, or physical conditioning. In time, as we evolve, and information like this is brought to the surface, it allows us to enter into realms we didn't know existed before, including the highest levels of performance.

THESE CONCEPTS AND PROCESSES WORK!

"Our challenges, year in and year out at USC, are to meet these extraordinarily high expectations and performance levels that we've set into motion years ago. To do that, we have to be tremendously strong mentally not to allow outside issues and expectations from keeping us from doing what we're capable of doing.

"That is our great challenge every year. So much of our success depends on the strength of our mindset and the strength of knowing ourselves and what we're all about. Winning the battle within is paramount to our program, and to our team reaching its highest levels of performance. I have used — and continue to use — all the lessons inside this book as a framework for building our mental game. Glen's concepts and processes work and I am thankful that they exist."

3

THE PERFECT
SWING IS THE ONE
YOU TRUST

Welcome to *Winning the Battle Within!* We're going to have some fun in this book, and, hopefully, along the way we'll share some tools and concepts that will help you lower your scores and enjoy this game to its fullest.

I've been lucky in my career to work with elite athletes in many sports, including more than fifty golfers who make their livings on the various professional tours around the world. But, truthfully, I get as much satisfaction and enjoyment out of helping high handicappers shave strokes off their scores as I do working with the pros. That's why the adventure we're about to take through these pages is designed to help golfers at all levels of ability.

People often ask me what makes *Winning the Battle Within* so different from traditional approaches to improving a player's golf game. In answering that question, I share with them the following true story.

Some years ago, a young man came to me and told me he had aspirations of playing on the PGA TOUR. I asked him what he thought he needed to do to improve his game so he could compete at that level.

"I need to find the technically perfect swing," he explained. "That's what all the great players have in common."

"Is that so?" I asked. "Exactly which technically perfect golf swing did you have in mind? The one Ernie Els uses? How about Arnold Palmer's? What about the ones used by Greg Norman, Jack Nicklaus, or Nick Price? Do those interest you?"

The young man's eyes narrowed and he looked at me suspiciously. He wasn't sure where I was going with these questions. I knew, of course, where he was going. He was in a dogged pursuit of the mythical Holy Grail that we, as a modern society of golfers, have created for ourselves. He was on a Great Quest for the perfect technical golf swing.

I could tell my questions weren't leading him any closer to the truth, so I shared with him the same thing I tell every player I work with, regardless of skill level.

"It's inside you already," I said. "The perfect swing is the one you trust."

The young man looked as though he had just swallowed a bumblebee. I may as well have told him his shoes were on fire. He wanted nothing more than to hot-foot it away from such blasphemy.

The young man was a good player, perhaps even good enough to challenge for a spot on the PGA TOUR. But he would not accept the simple concept that I had just shared with him. He refused to believe that there are many perfect swings. He chose, instead, to hold to what he had been taught to believe by every instructional golf book he had ever read and every video he had ever seen. He insisted that his success depended on finding a teacher who could show him how to make technically perfect moves throughout his swing. His quest ultimately took him elsewhere, and I never again heard of that young man.

At the same time, I was working with another young golfer, who had a very good technical swing, but like all good players, his swing was uniquely his own. He had been a standout high-school player, but had become uncertain of his game in college and had begun experimenting with a myriad of swing techniques. This mechanical approach slowed his progress, and he never shot low enough to consistently win a spot on his college golf team. When he first came to see me, he was selling golf apparel for a living. After college he nearly gave up golf, but found he loved the game too much to abandon his dreams. He rededicated himself to playing, and over the next year his belief in himself and his swing grew. He decided to give competitive golf another try. He came to me at that point, and I found him to be highly intellectual, intrigued by the mental aspects of the game. We began talking and working together with increasing regularity.

He loved the concept that trust, when combined with technique, is the most critical element in any golf swing. He understood that none of the great champions, from Bobby Jones and Ben Hogan to Jack Nicklaus and Tiger Woods, swung the golf club exactly the same way. While this young player continued to work on the technical aspects of his game, he worked even harder on the mental parts, especially the process that led him to an increasingly deep-seated trust in himself and his game.

Although he didn't have the amateur pedigree that some of the other players had, he began playing increasingly well because he had an important thing going for him—he trusted his swing and his game. His play sharpened and he became more successful, even winning some mini-tour events. He trusted himself enough to switch to a long putter long before it became a popular tool on the professional tours. Finally, he was ready for another run at 'Q School.' This time he relaxed, trusted his swing, and surprised more than a few observers by gaining his PGA touring card. He went on to great success, winning three PGA-TOUR events over the next few years. That player is Scott McCarron.

"Learning to trust my swing made my career possible," said Scott. "Glen and his innovative concepts about the inner game are a big reason I've been on the PGA TOUR for fourteen years."

Every Good Golfer is a 'Feel' Player

I tell these stories to illustrate the point that is at the core of this book and at the heart of everything I have learned in more than 40 years as a coach and an applied sport psychologist. As Scott and many other successful players will tell you, the perfect swing for you is the one you trust. The rest of this book is devoted to describing methods you can use to help build that trust within yourself.

Before I go any further, I want to address those of you with higher handicaps. If you are like a lot of my students, you may be asking, "How can I trust my swing when I know it's technically incorrect? Isn't this mental stuff for low handicappers and pros? Don't we have to learn technique first and trust second?"

The answer is that while those of you with mid to high handicaps can certainly benefit from improving the mechanics of your golf swings, you should do so while improving your mental games. Ideally, you should work on them together and in harmony with each other. Nothing I teach undervalues the importance of working with an enlightened swing coach. However, our technique-mad golfing culture tends to lead players into the trap of concentrating exclusively on the mechanical aspects of the golf swing. This single focus on technique not only robs golfers of their critical abilities to play in their imaginative minds, but also takes most of the fun out of the game. As professional golfers will tell you, every good player is a 'feel' player, and kinesthetic feel is in your imagination. Your improvement as a golfer is based as much on your mental abilities as on your physical skills.

You may find yourself somewhat resistant to this idea. That's because, in the past few decades, the golf industry has marketed equipment and technique as the keys to the game. The concept caught on because at its heart is a promise as addicting as a drug. *Pssst! Hey pal! All you need is the right magical technique or the newest piece of equipment, and you'll suddenly become a champion!* It's much easier, of course, to blame faulty technique or inferior equipment than to recognize a lack of trust in yourself.

Such quick-fix promises are central to our culture these days. At every turn, we are promised an easy solution—whether it is the newest dieting fad or the latest scheme to beat the stock market— but in truth, most of the promises are false, misleading, or temporary at best. The illusion that there is a perfect technical golf swing or that the newest miracle equipment will make you an instant winner is the golf industry's get-rich-quick scheme. But, the only people getting rich from this destructive myth are those who use it to sell equipment, lessons, videos, magazines, and gadgets.

I like to tease one of my lifetime friends, Ed Mayer, about being a great example of an equipment junkie. Ed, like thousands of other golfers, purchases every driver that promises an extra 20 yards and constantly seeks the latest set of forgiving irons. Yet, Ed's game remains the same. I've told him that when I retire, I plan to spend the first six months selling clubs from his garage, and even then I will not have exhausted his supply. No one on my long list of golfing buddies is more fun to play with than Ed, and I know he will laugh and agree with me when he reads this. His passionate commitment to this challenging game is unparalleled, but his improvement awaits the day he stops buying clubs and starts trusting his swing.

As Eric Jones, the 2003 Masters Long-Drive champion and teaching professional in the San Francisco Bay Area, so aptly put it, "New clubs, shafts, launch monitors, and so on have improved certain aspects of my game, but none so much as simply trusting my swing and using my imagination."

McCarron once told me that he talked to a 17-handicapper who expressed doubt that trusting his swing would do any good until he had learned better technique. "I don't buy that one bit," Scott said, chuckling. "That's why he's a 17-handicapper. If he'd work only on his mental game, he'd drop to a 13 in a short time."

One of my favorite professionals, one who plays within his imaginative mind at all times, is Fred Couples. While I will admit that Fred is at the far end of the imaginative spectrum, he once said something about swing techniques that I have never forgotten. It makes me laugh to remember it, but the sentiment within Freddy's statement is really the essence of why he rose to the top of his profession, winning the Masters in 1992 and becoming the number one player in the world. Fred, of course, has a unique swing, but it was one he learned to trust implicitly when he was tearing up the PGA TOUR in the early 1990's.

"As far as swing technique is concerned, I don't know did-dly-squat," Fred once said. "When I'm playing well, I don't even take aim."

Ray Floyd was another champion who trusted his unique swing and became one of the best players in the world. "If a great golf swing puts you high on the money list, some of us would be broke," Floyd said.

The legendary Bobby Jones was one of the first great players to talk about the importance of the mental game, particularly shot-making visualization as opposed to mechanical-swing thoughts. "You swing your best when you have the fewest things to think about," Jones mused.

Sam Snead once said, "Thinking instead of acting is the number one golf disease." Few players were better in the clutch than

Lee Trevino. Yet, Lee's own assessment of his swing was that it was far from perfect. "Are you kidding?" he said. "My swing is so bad I look like a caveman killing his lunch." Tiger Woods, Jim Furyk, Annika Sorenstam, Vijay Singh, Michelle Wie, Sergio Garcia, Natalie Gulbis, Darrin Clarke, Michael Campbell, Allen Doyle, and especially Jack Nicklaus are examples of wonderful players who have come to trust their own individual swings.

My point is that it is not a 'perfect' technical swing that makes a champion or allows amateurs to permanently improve and drop their handicaps. It is something quite different. It is, in a word, trust. Trust leads to confidence, and confidence leads to the rhythmic, synchronized completion of your backswing, down-swing, and follow through. Trusting your swing produces more quality shots, better scores, greater enjoyment, and ultimately leads to the winner's circle.

Winning the Battle Within is about how to gain that trust even if, like Freddy, you don't know 'diddly-squat' about technique. It's about providing you with the keys to a powerful mental state that will enable you to get the most out of yourself and your ability. Learning to understand and trust your own unique swing through a disciplined process is the foundation of consistent performance.

4

THE POWER
OF SUSPENDING
JUDGMENT

Winning is an obsession with Americans. We've been taught since we were young that winning isn't the most important thing, it is the only thing. As a society, we reward winners in every way possible, from financial gains to a communal respect that sometimes borders on adulation.

Winning was certainly important to me as I grew up playing sports, and then later during my early coaching career. I was all about winning. I wanted my teams to compete and win more than anything.

Who knows exactly where our competitive nature comes from—perhaps it is as ancient a part of human nature as survival itself. Perhaps, like a lot of adolescent boys and girls, I was looking for approval from my parents, especially my father. It took me until I was an adult, and well into my coaching career, to learn that my Father would love me whether my teams won or lost. Perhaps we also seek recognition and even an identity through winning, or it may be the promise of the riches found in the winner's circle. Whatever the reason, it's easy to see why we are so obsessed with winning.

More to Life

An intriguing thing happened, though, as I grew older. As my teams won championships, I began to realize that it wasn't winning alone that attracted me to sports; I was intrigued by the process of practice, preparation, and performance. I had expanded my life to include a wife and family, and after some time it became clear to me that there was much more to life than simply winning an athletic contest. At the same time, I began to appreciate sports and performance in a more profound way than ever before. My studies during the human-potential movement of the 1960's and 70's helped me realize that to reach the true center of any sport, especially golf, you have to move beyond merely being obsessed with winning. *Golf in the Kingdom,* with its multitude of subtle, beautiful messages about golf, life, joy, and trust, helped clarify this and focus my personal growth beyond a fixation with winning. I picked up the novel in 1973, and soon after reading it, I was reunited with my boyhood friend and author, Michael Murphy. The reading and subsequent inspiring collaborations with Michael forever changed my view of sports. Numerous other readings from humanistic-psychology and philosophy libraries added to the lessons in Murphy's classic. Among my favorites are Tim Gallwey's *Inner Game of Tennis,* George Leonard's *The Ultimate Athlete,* Ellen Gerber's *Sport and the Body,* and Eugene Herrigal's *Zen and the Art of Archery*—all timeless examinations of the inner world of sport performance.

Please don't misunderstand me. I enjoy winning, but I have the most fun competing when both sides are fully engaged and playing as hard as they can to win. I like what NBA-all-star Bill Russell said in his book, *Second Wind:* "The most memorable moments in my NBA career were not the 11 championships, but the few times, often for just a quarter, when a few players on the court would get hot, and their heat would spread to others and the whole game would 'levitate.' The games were so absorbing and so intense that it made no difference who won or lost."

I still play in golf tournaments in Northern California when I can, and I try to play my best game every time. The best times for me, though, are the stretches of play, much like Russell's reminiscence, when everything and everyone is clicking, the competition is intense, momentum swings back and forth, trusting swings emerge, and humor flourishes. I savor those moments. The three days of camaraderie and competition during the Fall River Invitational, a tournament I host at a priceless jewel of a course (Fall River Golf and Country Club) in the northeastern corner of Northern California, is the time I relish the most.

Over the years, I've learned that whether you win or lose, a variety of important benefits can be gleaned from every competition. In fact, if you evaluate your performance without judgment and with awareness and a keen eye into the inner corridors of your mind, you learn as much about yourself and your performance when you lose as when you win. Insightful discoveries are abundant when the mind is totally aware and free from judgment. You want to win every time you put a club in your hand, but that is only part of the story. You will reach your top mental performance level when you begin to understand that competing as fully as you can, regardless of whether you win or lose, will provide you with a deep sense of satisfaction. Too often, we don't allow ourselves to taste that wonderful elixir unless we win. We don't allow ourselves to experience the joy of competing intensely, and by not doing so, in the long run, we rob ourselves of enthusiasm, trust, motivation, and the opportunity to learn. You may lose the day, but you will never lose the lesson.

Suspending Judgment

In my experience with the inner game of golf, I have found that this is a major key to sustaining feelings of joy and satisfaction and to promoting steady improvement. The major change required of most of us is to become more nonjudgmental about our games and ourselves. The great players of today know this. As I was writing this chapter and reflecting on self-judgment, Annika Sorenstam was attempting to make golfing history by becoming the first LPGA player ever to win six consecutive tournaments. Even winning two tournaments in a row is a monumental achievement. Winning six in row would have been one of the great feats in golfing history. Annika, who is clearly one of the world's elite athletes and as advanced mentally as any player in history, is among the few golfers currently capable of such an accomplishment.

In May 2005, she opened her quest for her sixth win at the Michelob Ultra Open in Williamsburg, Virginia, with a disappointing 76. It was the first time in 44 straight rounds she had been over par. It was clear Annika had finally let down, perhaps under the self-imposed pressure of trying to win her sixth tournament in a row. She had the opportunity to use that as an excuse, and nearly everyone would have accepted it from her. Most golfers would have complained of being tired and would have pointed immediately at their five previous victories. It was a perfect time for excuses.

But, it is not an accident that Annika is among the best players ever to play the game. This is how she responded to shooting the 76: "I don't know what to say about this round. I thought I played pretty good today. It just didn't go my way. I just want to move forward and go low for the next three days, and I know I can do it."

Impressive response wasn't it? It was a complete self-affirmation of her abilities, and there was no doubt Annika believed exactly what she said. Her last words may be the six most important words in any competitor's vocabulary: "I know I can do it." What that tells me, and this has been evident with Annika for years, is that she enjoys the game. She loves playing and competing. I am firmly convinced that enjoyment begins precisely at the moment when players stop judging themselves so harshly. What did Annika say when she shot her highest score in 44 rounds? "I thought I played pretty good today. It just didn't go my way."

Annika did not win the tournament, but when interviewed afterwards, she took responsibility for her round. "I simply didn't play my best," she said. "I'll just have to go out and start another streak."

The story doesn't end there. The following week, she played in the Chick-Fil-A Charity Championship (a regular LPGA-TOUR stop) in Stockridge, Georgia. She shot 67-64-67-67 to win the tournament by a whopping ten strokes for her 60th career win on the LPGA TOUR. Annika's amazingly strong mental attitude allows her to get the most out of her game. She has all the shots and is a superb ball-striker, but her true strength is in her powerful mental game. Perhaps no golfer in the game today has a more seamless inner game than Annika.

Ruthless Self-Judging is Destructive

As I mentioned, one of the primary keys to Annika's success is how much she enjoys the game. She refuses to allow bad breaks or mental pressures to erode that enjoyment. She knows that over time the breaks will even out. The lesson embedded in all this is that learning to enjoy yourself on the golf course is critical to long-term, high-level performance. Finding the joy in your game will help make you a better player. Ruthless self-judgment (and judgment of others, especially of our playing partners) will kill that joy faster than following a slow foursome on a hot day. Men, especially, have to overcome the feeling that harsh self-judgment is somehow a positive, masculine thing to do. It isn't. It's destructive and useless. Woods and Els don't do it. Nicklaus and Palmer didn't do it either. It is critically important for you to make a conscious and determined effort to begin to take the self-judgment out of your game.

Kathy DeBoer, an elite basketball and volleyball player and a high-level volleyball coach before becoming an associate athletic director at the University of Kentucky, in *Gender Differences in Sport and the Workplace,* makes an interesting observation. She writes that one of the most important skills that men in sport must learn is how to lose without making ill-intentioned self-judgments. I agree with her. Men need to understand that losing is not the end of their lives or their virility. Losing must be understood, instead, as a great opportunity to learn. If we can learn to lose without judgment, then we have a chance to move on to play another day, to continue to learn and improve, and eventually to enter the winner's circle.

Pete Carroll on Suspending Judgment

Pete has a rationale for suspending judgment that I find most profound. In typical fashion, he goes right to the heart of things, and you'll see how his take on the art of suspending judgment runs parallel to Annika's version and promotes the building of self-confidence. Here's the Pete-Carroll antidote to ruthless self-judgment, and I think it is a good one:

"What you want to do is suspend judgment on your round and on any given shot for as long as possible," said Pete. "Don't say that you are having a good day or a bad day. Suspend that judgment. If you've made three birdies in a row and you've never made four birdies in a row, don't think about making that fourth birdie—just concentrate on your next shot. Just keep walking. Passing judgment causes you to choke. You won't choke if you go from moment to moment, from play to play, from drill to drill, from repetition to repetition, all the time focusing only on the next thing that is in front of you. You must have short-term vision. It's like the lens of a camera. What's right in front of you will be clear, unless you begin to focus on something far in the background. When you do that, what is nearest to you—the next shot—will go out of focus. Once you start thinking about your score and how your score will be judged, you have suddenly focused your camera way out there, and your concentration on your next shot will get fuzzy. Don't write your victory speech before you have hit all the shots. Suspending judgment is not always easy, but with the proper practice and on-course routines, it can be done."

Pete proved true to his philosophy after his team's tough 2006 loss to the Texas University Longhorns in the Rose Bowl for the national championship. He refused to blame his players or his coaches, saying that his team didn't run out of heart, they only ran out of time. He also praised the Longhorns, which showed not only a great deal of class, but also that he stayed true to his beliefs.

In similar fashion, in the locker room, after a surprising defeat at Oregon State in 2008, which could have been a devastating loss, the team began focus on their next practice almost immediately.

Judgment by Others

When we combine judgment from others with ruthless self-judgment, we create an insidiously destructive mix. The fact is, we will be judged by others no matter what we do. But, we can't control what others think. We can only control how we respond to others' untimely judgments. This kind of control—thoughts and responses—is ultimately how we take charge of our performance.

Part of winning the battle within is focusing solely on the things we can control and letting everything else go. Imagine yourself on a sleek, high-performance boat on a fast-moving river. You can't control what flotsam and jetsam may drift by you in that river, but you can make sure your boat is shipshape and watertight. Your survival on the river depends not on what floats by you beyond your control, but on how you maintain your craft. Ultimately, the seaworthiness of your own vessel should be your only concern. Whether you float or sink on the golf course depends largely upon how effectively you suspend self-judgment and play down judgment from others.

First-Nationwide-Tour-winner Tyler Williamson reflected on an experience he had as a caddie at the PGA-TOUR finals in 2005. (He narrowly missed advancing himself.) Tyler realized that as a caddie he had no recourse but to suspend judgment, even after the worst of missed shots by his player. As a caddie, after the shot, he moved briskly to the next shot, paced off the yardage, determined the lie, wind, pin placement, etc, and gave the information to his player. His language was task specific ("It's 162 yards to the pin.") and supportive ("You can do it! Stay on task!"). Realizing that he could do the same for himself when playing was an important discovery for Tyler. He knew that a caddie who deviates from task-specific and supportive language and behavior will soon have no bag to carry. Similarly, if a player doesn't suspend judgment and re-focus, making cuts will remain out of reach and winning will be but a dream.

5

PLAYING WITH IMAGINATION

Early one morning on a recent cruise to Mazatlán, Mexico, I was sitting alone on the deck, writing material for an upcoming *Winning-the-Battle-Within* workshop. The air was calm, and dolphins were playing in the ocean off the side of the ship. Their actions seemed to be steeped in the pure joy of movement; they were, at that moment, perfect athletes. I was lost in thought, when a newly acquired friend, Sam, sat down next to me and asked me what I was doing. During prior conversations, Sam and I had found common interests in three areas—jazz, sports, and entertainment performance. I told him I was probing into the deeper meaning of performance and determining ways to explain, in my workshops, how giving up conscious control of a golf swing allows a player to gain control.

"What I'm working on," I said, "is a way of explaining the process that players must go through to move from the conscious mind to the mind of imagination. I want to explain how players must begin to 'feel' and 'see' their swings, because that is the clearest path to trusting your swing. I am keying on how important it is to play the game in your imagination."

Although Sam had little experience in sports other than as a spectator, he was aware of the challenges of performance because he was a conductor of jazz musicians. He thought for a long moment and watched the dolphins. Then he said, "I think I know what you mean. There is the jazz that most musicians play and then there is the jazz of Thelonious Monk. The other musicians are good technicians and skillful at what they do—but Thelonious Monk swings."

I laughed, because I immediately understood Sam's metaphor for imaginative performance. It was not to undervalue the playing of the other musicians, but rather to more clearly define the improvisational nature of jazz musicians, like Monk, who play intuitive riffs that transcend fundamental, piano-playing mechanics. Thelonious Monk's improvisations are based on the skill of moving from a sound foundation of technique in the rational mind to their ultimate creative form in the imaginative mind.

Top golfers undergo the same process on a regular basis. But, even recreational golfers can experience this creative state. Players like Tiger Woods, Phil Mickelson, Jack Nicklaus, Arnold Palmer, Annika Sorenstam, Scott McCarron, Jeff Brehaut, Charlie Wi and Kirk Triplett all understand the importance of technique as the foundation for improvisational golf. But, they also know there is a higher level of consciousness for players than the conscious mind. Technique, which includes attention to details such as swing plane, grip, stance, setup, alignment, posture, and ball position, is critical to playing good golf; however, top performance demands something more, and all golfers, regardless of skill level, are capable of playing in this higher-consciousness frame, if they will only allow themselves to do so.

Lawrence Meredith, a fellow professor at the University of the Pacific and the author of *Life Before Death: A Spiritual Journey of*

Mind and Body, has been a friend and inspiration to me for years. He describes the imaginative mind as the "ability to create sensory coherence...looking at possible ways for all these (sensory data) to be organized...The imagination not only recognizes but actually creates novel order." It allows golfers and musicians alike to sense the movements or improvisational riffs in advance and automatically place them in synchronous order.

In this chapter, I want to explain further what it means to play in the imaginative mind. Many players prefer to think of golf as a scientific game, played in the cerebral cortex—a conscious, technical, linear sport. In truth, it is just the opposite. While technique and conscious thought play a vital role, the game, at its highest levels, is played much as dolphins swim in the sea and Thelonious Monk plays the piano—in the improvisational or imaginative mind, unfettered by conscious thought.

All of this goes toward learning to trust your swing. You can't trust an athletic movement when your mind is full of technical and conscious thoughts. It would be like Michelangelo painting by the numbers, Frank Lloyd Wright designing tract homes, or Stan Getz playing "Chopsticks" with Oscar Peterson. To play consistent, quality golf and enjoy it, you must learn that gaining control of your swing comes through letting go of your conscious thoughts. This seeming contradiction formed the basis of my musings on the ship deck that morning off the coast of Mexico, and I realized that it was critical, in this book, to explain how to make the transfer during performance from the conscious mind to the automatic or imaginative mind. This is perhaps the most important step in changing the way you understand and play the game. The imaginative mind is not only where top performances are born, it is where the true inner joy of the game is found.

Let 'Nothingness' into Your Shots

Perhaps no one expressed this concept better than my lifelong friend, Michael Murphy, when he wrote *Golf in the Kingdom*. Michael wrote about playing golf with the mythical pro of Burning Bush Golf Links in Scotland and protagonist of the novel, Shivas Irons. Michael, an excellent player, was struggling and had just carded a double-bogey after hitting one into the ocean. He was sitting on a rock looking at the waves when Shivas came over and laid a hand on his shoulder.

"'Ye try too hard, and ye think too much,' Shivas said with the authority that Scottish golf professionals often assume. 'Why don't ye go wi' yer pretty swing? Let nothingness into yer shots.'

"'I suppose he knew I was losing heart,' Michael wrote. 'His words made me feel better. It did seem silly to ruin all the beautiful scenery with the fuss I was making.'"

The mantra in this chapter is Shivas's inveiglement to Michael: "Let nothingness into yer shots." Indeed, that may well be the single best piece of advice any golfer can receive.

The Imaginative Mind

Before I go any further, I want to fully explain what it means to "let nothingness into your shots" and play in the imaginative mind. Our imaginative minds are full of imagery, feeling, intuition, and sensory receptors. We connect with the environment through our senses rather than through our conscious minds. In terms of performance, especially with respect to golf, this means turning off the flow of information about the technical aspects of our swings that wants to flood in from the conscious mind. The problem with this technical information is that it overpowers the imagery and sensory nature of the imaginative mind. Sensory information— visualization, feel, sound and touch—are required to reach top performance. When was the last time you hit a good shot without 'seeing' it in your mind's eye or 'feeling' it before you swung? Believe me, no professional golfer I've ever known has won a tournament while thinking about technique on every swing. Top performances are always linked directly to positive imagery.

"Golf is first a game of seeing and feeling....It demands a stillness of mind and sensitivity to all that is around you....Golf is a game for listening to the messages from within...and once you have paid attention, it becomes a doorway to marvelous realms," writes Murphy in *The Kingdom of Shivas Irons*.

All enlightened technical instructors know this. They know the importance of what they teach, but they also know that technique is best carried out through the imaginative mind. Dave Pelz is one of the most famous short-game instructors in the world, in part because he understands the process required for great performance.

"Great golfers don't think; they just feel," Pelz said recently. "The pros imagine the shot they want to hit, then their minds let their bodies do what their bodies already know how to do. The best players see what they want to do before they do it. They don't think about mechanics, they just feel the swing they want."

McCarron on the Imaginative Mind

Scott and I have had long talks about the critical nature of playing in the imaginative mind. Here are some of the valuable insights he shared with me:

"Playing in the imaginative mind is something that has to be done before you can reach your potential as a golfer," Scott said. "Playing in the imaginative mind is being creative. When you walk up to a shot, it just comes to you, whether you want to hit it high or low, fade it, draw it, or just hit it straight. It's about getting technical-swing thoughts out of the way, so you can see the flight of the golf ball. It's about feeling the swing. I know I play my best when I have no swing thoughts; I'm just being creative, feeling the swing and its rhythm. When I want to draw it, I don't think about doing anything, I just do it. If you've practiced correctly, your body will know how to react. It will do what you have imagined."

I stopped Scott at that point. "That's undeniably true for you, but you are a highly successful professional on the PGA TOUR," I said. "Do you think it is also true for higher handicappers?"

Scott nodded. "No doubt about it," he said in his typical, positive manner. "Higher handicappers need to think that way, too. It doesn't mean they will hit shots as consistently as lower handicappers will. But, if they play in the imaginative mind on a consistent basis, there is no question they will play better golf. I always like to say, 'If you have an 18 handicapper, and he's going out to play golf today, he should be thinking as well or better than I do when I go out to play.' That doesn't mean he is going to shoot 72, but he might shoot 5 under his handicap. He certainly isn't going to do any good, if he's thinking about the technical aspects of his golf swing."

Scott and I are of similar minds when it comes to addressing why so many golfers think constantly about technique. "Hey, we're all technocrats these days," he said, shaking his head. "You see golf swings analyzed everywhere. They're analyzed in newspapers, in golf magazines, on the Golf Channel, and in every telecast of every tournament. Everybody, it seems, is in the business of analyzing golf swings. Every time you see a professional golfer mis-hit a shot on television, some analyst immediately starts telling you what technically went wrong with his swing. I always want to say, 'Hey, wait a minute! Maybe the guy just didn't trust that particular swing. Maybe he held on too long because he didn't commit mentally to the shot. Maybe he didn't buy into his strategy. Maybe he allowed technique to intrude into his imaginative mind, and that caused doubt to creep in just as he swung.' Frankly, those are the real reasons players miss shots. The analysts are giving the audience what it has come to expect—a technical analysis. More often than not there isn't anything wrong with the guy's swing—he just didn't trust it that one time."

What the Pros Say

I have found that, without exception, the touring professionals I work with are convinced that playing in the imaginative mind is critical to their success.

"It's absolutely important," says Matt Hansen, the brilliant young player from northern California who won the 2004 Monterey Bay Open before qualifying for the 2006 PGA Tour. "The more I get into the imaginative mind, the better I play," said Matt. "I can see and feel exactly what I'm going to do. When I see my shot before I hit it, that's when I play my best. I become so engrossed in the creative aspects that everything else is blocked out."

Triplett agrees. "You have to get there if you want to play consistent, top-flight golf," he said. "The more you play in your imaginative mind, the more comfortable you'll be with it. Sometimes it just happens naturally, but most of us were taught to block out our imaginative minds in favor of thinking mechanically, that is, about swing technique. Successful, consistent golfers are able to process the conscious, technical side of the game and then move on into playing by feel. All I know is that every time I've played really well, in the zone, I've not been worried about any mechanics. I just look at the hole and say, 'Here comes another birdie!'"

It may almost sound as if these highly accomplished golfers play with nary a thought in their heads. In fact, just the opposite is true—they are intensely engaged in the process, constantly sifting and evaluating information like lie, stance, wind, moisture, distance, trajectory, target, and ball flight. But, when it's time to swing, great players forget about mechanics and rely on what their imaginative minds tell them is the right shot for the conditions.

An International Perspective

Some of the more fascinating discussions I have had on this subject took place with Nick Ushijima, a fine amateur player from Japan, and Herbert Forster, the former German mens' champion who played for the University of the Pacific golf team a few years ago. Herbert, who is now a businessman and educator based in Germany where he is offering *Winning-the-Battle-Within* workshops, remains fascinated with the concept of playing in the imaginative mind.

"It is such a different idea than any of us were exposed to growing up in Germany," said Herbert. "There, it's all about mechanics. Nearly every professional stresses nothing but mechanics. This is probably to be expected, since Germany is known for being so oriented toward engineering, and efficiency and precision are so tied to the German image. That approach was all I ever encountered until I went to The University of the Pacific and met Glen. I happened to be at a place in my life and my golf career that I was wide open to his ideas. I had reached a point where all the work I had put into my game was no longer paying off. I had gone as far as I could go. Something was missing. In the beginning, I didn't know what Glen meant when he talked about playing in the imaginative mind. It sounded fanciful to me, at first. It took time for me to grasp his concepts, and they didn't change my game overnight, but in the long run, they made a huge difference. Not only did I begin to play better, I began to enjoy golf much more. Without question, Glen's ideas are badly needed in Germany and other countries. Not only would golfers improve their games, I firmly believe that people would improve their lives by including some of these concepts in their daily habits."

Japan Open to New Approach

Ushijima said much the same thing about Japan. "Generally speaking, Japanese golfers tend to be very mechanical compared to Americans, and Americans are pretty mechanical in their approach," he said. "One of the reasons Japanese golfers are so mechanical is that they spend so much time on the driving ranges instead of the courses. But, there is also an important cultural influence in that form is very important for the Japanese. This is true for all Japanese traditions, such as judo, kendo, karate, etc. The first thing a student must learn is form, rather than the practical way of fighting or defending. This mind-set is carried over to golf, because proper form is much more deeply rooted in the society than most people would think."

Ushijima thought for a moment and then added, "That said, contemporary top Japanese athletes, including golfers, are becoming more westernized. An increasing number of coaches are bringing in different ideas. Your ideas, Glen, on the imaginative mind would be tremendously helpful to most Japanese golfers. I think many are beginning to become open to these new ideas. Sport science and sport psychology are hot topics in Japan."

Emotional Intelligence and Our Three Minds

In order to operate more fully in your imaginative mind, it is helpful to understand that there are three distinct minds in which we process information—the conscious, emotional, and imaginative minds. Each has a significantly different effect on performance.

Motor skills, such as swinging a golf club, should be learned through a process that includes all three minds, but should be performed only from the imaginative mind. (I have borrowed ideas from Daniel Goleman, author of *Emotional Intelligence* and the psychology editor for *The New York Times*. The adaptations of the concepts of the three minds to golf are my own.)

The conscious mind is occupied with intellectual reasoning and conscious thought. This is the mind that should be utilized for developing strategy for golf performance. It is best used when the body is in a static state—in other words, when we aren't attempting an athletic movement such as swinging a golf club. The conscious mind loves technique, strategy, and course-management skills, but it gets confused when the body is in physical motion. It is best activated in a quiet time before the round to develop a smart approach to playing a specific course. It should also be clicked on for a moment during pre-shot routines to help absorb all the information needed from the environment. We need to know things like the kind of lie, which way the wind is blowing, which side of the hole to putt from, and how far it is to the center of the green.

The conscious mind is great for collecting this type of information.

The emotional mind is a different creature altogether. It doesn't collect information; rather, it reacts to it and to different stimuli. It produces emotions such as anger, disappointment, anxiety, sadness, frustration, and of course, happiness and joy. The emotional mind, as we all know from experience, is the most powerful mind. It works the fastest, and can be something of a bully. When activated at full strength, it shuts down both the conscious and imaginative minds. Think of your worst rounds in recent memory, and you'll probably find that they occurred when your emotional mind was overpowering the other two. Often, golfers (especially non-professionals) bring an overbearing emotional mind to the golf course with them, laden with worries or anxieties from work, home, or other parts of their lives. In short, the emotional mind packs a powerful punch that has to be kept in balance during performance.

It's important to realize that, as Goleman says, "The start-up of a negative emotion can't always be controlled. The direction, intensity, and duration can be." My colleague, Eric Jones, expresses the same idea in a slightly different way: "You can't always control the immediate, almost instinctive, reaction of anger, disgust, frustration, or other emotions to a mis-hit shot. But, you are in total control of whether that emotion makes it to the surface in your expressions or actions, whether you let the emotion consume you or you let it go, and whether you let that emotion linger to affect your next shot."

You can manage your emotional mind most effectively through 'mindfulness,' which is a Zen term for total awareness in the present. Translated, it simply means gaining knowledge of yourself and staying in the present so that you can monitor your emotions, learn techniques for identifying harmful ones, and cut them off before they negatively affect your performance.

John White at the HeartMath Institute in Boulder Creek, California, says that well-documented research regarding the harmful aspects of negative emotions, indicates that, "The rush of secretions brought on by volatile emotions limits muscular control." The Institute believes you can learn to reverse the negative energy created by these volatile emotions and channel them into a force for consistent performance. If you want to manage your emotions under pressure do what McCarron, Wi, Hansen and many others do and utilize the emWave (Personal Stress Reliever) technology to learn more about monitoring your emotions. Once you're able to reach a coherent emotional state in a quiet setting, the next step is to transfer it to your pre, post and in between shot routines. The HeartMath Institute (HeartMath.com) presents programs for mental and emotional management across numerous domains in business and all forms of performance.

Managing your emotional mind doesn't mean you must have the coolness of Fred Couples, the intensity of Tiger Woods, or the mental toughness of Annika Sorenstam. It means identifying your own individual strengths, learning to be yourself, and playing your own game. It also involves developing and practicing your own great-performance profile, which we'll explore later.

Knowing when to apply your conscious mind and managing the enormous power of your emotional mind will allow you to more easily enter and remain in the imaginative mind while you perform.

Some people call the imaginative mind the 'athletic mind,' which is a state of consciousness (or unconsciousness) that allows your body a total freedom of movement, reaction, and improvisation that cannot exist if the conscious mind is fully active. Can you imagine LaBron James getting to the top of his jump shot and wondering if the positioning of his hands on the basketball is correct before he lets it fly toward the basket? If he did that very often, he would end up one of the tallest people in the unemployment line, because he wouldn't stay in the NBA very long. Or picture Randy Johnson getting ready to release a 97-mile-per-hour fastball and suddenly wondering if his right knee is aligning correctly with his left elbow. I wouldn't want to be in the batter's box if Johnson were thinking these things, because his control would be dubious at best. He and every other elite athlete know that you cannot properly perform athletically if you are thinking mechanically during the actual motion of the activity. Certainly, using your conscious mind at times is critical in order to prepare properly. Watching game films, for example, is the perfect time for full activation of the conscious mind. Developing a course-management strategy for Augusta National for the next time you qualify for the Masters is a great time to apply your conscious mind. (Okay, so we all don't get to play Augusta, but what about developing a solid management strategy for your favorite course?)

Generally, your conscious mind works best when your body is not doing anything complicated. It absorbs and processes information most efficiently when you are at rest. At the same time, your body in movement will be most efficient when your conscious mind is at rest. The conscious mind plays a vital role in the process of learning a new skill, but not in actually performing that skill.

For example, a peculiar thing happens during live theater that every experienced actor knows about. Actors must not only learn their lines, they also must learn what actions they will take on stage as they say each line. This action sequencing is called 'blocking.' Each line delivered is coordinated with a movement and practiced that way. Illustrative of the delicate relationship between kinesthetic movement and the conscious mind is the fact that even veteran actors are likely to immediately forget their lines if the blocking is suddenly changed. In other words, if an actor has prepared to shout, "To be or not to be!" as he is walking toward one side of the stage, he is likely to stumble over the line (well, maybe not that line) if he suddenly, and without preparation, is forced to walk to the opposite side of the stage while delivering the line. There can be no doubt that to achieve peak efficiency, the mind must be free of conscious or technical thoughts during any type of athletic performance.

The Power of 'Simple'

Playing golf in the imaginative mind requires more than the absence of technical thoughts. It requires the collaboration of your senses. You must be visually aware of the target, the ball flight, and your own swing. It requires kinesthetic awareness of your body position, balance, swing plane, and tempo. It also requires an anticipatory, auditory awareness of a well-struck shot or of the ball falling into the cup after a center-cut putt. Finally, it requires a tactile awareness of the feel of the club as it strikes through the ball and pulls you into a well-balanced finishing position.

As Murphy writes: "Hear the inner sounds and rhythms, and let them enter your play. Golf is first a game of seeing and feeling. It can teach you stillness of mind and sensitivity to the textures of wind and green."

If I could encapsulate this inner-game concept into one word, it would be 'simplify.' The process I'm talking about is one of simplifying the game to the basic elements of seeing, feeling, and hearing good shots. These are the fundamental components of an uncomplicated game made complicated by our conscious thoughts and by an industry that would have us believe that the secret of golf lies deep in the exacting fields of geometry, physics, and chemistry.

"An image in our mind can become an irresistible path," writes Murphy. "Let go of ordinary feeling and thought, and you are at once more self-sufficient."

Three Stages of Motor Learning

Hopefully, right now you're feeling a little optimistic, but perhaps you're a bit frustrated, too. That's because so far I've only laid out the general aspects of the concepts embedded in *Winning the Battle Within*. We're about to get to the active, how-to parts of this process—the specific techniques you can learn to help you properly align and balance your conscious, emotional, and imaginative minds. This balance is a healthful, powerful, and amazingly productive thing to achieve. It is the fastest and most direct pathway to better, more consistent performance.

Learning an Athletic Skill

As we launch into this process, it is important to remind ourselves of the three steps to learning any athletic skill. Some scientists call these 'motor learning stages.' You probably already know these three steps, so just consider this a quick refresher. *Motor Learning and Performance,* by Richard Schmidt, contains the clearest discussion of learning stages I've seen.

The first step in learning a new physical movement is called the 'cognitive phase.' In this phase, most learning takes place in the conscious mind. Through it, we absorb new information, such as the proper grip, stance, step-up, takeaway, transition move, and follow-through of a golf swing. This is the proper time to activate the conscious mind fully. We listen, watch, and learn. When we do execute a swing, trying out our new knowledge, the feedback we receive is external. Someone (hopefully an enlightened teacher) tells us whether or not we've correctly performed what we've just learned. This is the conscious part of the learning process. But conscious learning is rarely smooth; rather, it is full of starts, stops, and questions. If we're learning to dance, we're likely to step on the instructor's toes during this stage.

The second step is called the 'associative phase.' During this phase, we take our dance instructor for a little whirl around the floor, perhaps surprising her (or him) with a bit of show and flourish now and then. Golfwise, we begin to swing with accuracy and consistency. The swing begins to come more naturally, but there is still a bit of conscious thought involved. Many of our shots soar straight and true, but some still make spectators duck and cover. We're not ready for prime time yet, but we are getting it. This is the stage where we might turn to our instructor, before the instructor gives any external feedback, and say, "I'm beginning to feel it."

Finally, the third step is the 'autonomous phase.' As the term implies, performance becomes automatic. Through proper practice and an understanding that the conscious mind must now retreat completely to the sidelines, athletes put into motion all that has been learned. They immerse themselves in their imaginative minds, with senses and feelings replacing process and analysis. It's only in this state that athletes can get into the zone and perform at top levels. Most teachers and successful athletes agree that the most important factor in achieving this state is proper practice, which allows trust to replace the conscious mind during performance. How long it takes to arrive at automatic play depends upon the enlightenment of the instructor, the complexity of the skill, and the golfer's willingness to practice.

By now, I hope you are convinced that playing in the imaginative mind is critical to playing good, consistent golf. Let's move on to some specific steps you can take to put yourself in better balance, both mentally and physically.

6

THE S.A.T. PROCESS:

Five Seconds That Will Change Your Game

I want to initiate our journey toward winning the battle within in what might seem like an unusual way—not with a pre-shot routine, as many books do, but with a post-shot routine. I'm presenting it to you early in this book because it is unique and powerful, and something that you can immediately build into your game to enhance your play and make your rounds much more enjoyable. I designed it with the help of top players and colleagues who have embraced it as a key instrument in their search for trust and confidence. Some touring professionals, including McCarron, Triplett, Charlie Wi and others, now consider it their "fifteenth club." We call it the golf 'S.A.T. Process.' (I'll explain in a moment how it got its name.)

In summary, this process, which takes only seconds to perform, is a post-shot routine that allows you to quickly discover the cause of an errant shot and immediately replace the image and feel with the image and feel that you want. This prevents you from falling into patterns of mis-hit shots and greatly reduces the number of errant shots you're likely to hit in a round. It also gives you more control of yourself and your game.

Review, Replace, and Refocus

One of the tremendous benefits of the S.A.T. Process is that it helps you shake off the negative emotions that attend an errant shot while allowing you to properly prepare for your next shot. Let's say you just hit a high fade into the deep rough. In the past, you've probably allowed feelings of disgust and anger to take over and you may even have slammed your club into the turf. What the S.A.T. Process allows you to do is systematically get rid of those negative feelings and instantly replace them with a positive emotion, feel and image.

As my friend Ken Ravizza, a sport psychologist at California State University at Fullerton, says, this kind of process allows athletes to "review, replace, and refocus." Ravizza has worked with a wide range of elite athletes, including the NCAA 2005 champion baseball team from California State University at Fullerton, the Los Angeles Angels baseball team, the U.S. men's water polo team, and the football team at the University of Nebraska. "To reach their full potential, all athletes need a developed methodology for reviewing, replacing, and refocusing on what they want to do," he said.

The Three Reasons Golfers Mis-hit Shots

To fully understand how the S.A.T. Process works, it's important to understand that there are three primary reasons, or a combination thereof as to why we mis-hit shots. Errant shots are nearly always caused by a breakdown in *strategy, aim, or trust*. I'll go into more detail on each of these three reasons toward the end of this chapter, but let's take a quick look at them for now. Let's start with strategy. If you think about it for a moment, it is astounding how often golfers fail to commit to their own strategies. Think back to the times you've heard a fellow player moan that he or she should have used a different club after missing a shot. How many times have we done it ourselves?

The second reason for errant shots is incorrect aim. PGA-TOUR players say this is one of the most common mistakes they make—misaligning feet, hips, or shoulders to the target line. Aiming your body, mind, and clubface to the target correctly is essential to good ball flight. Aim is a constant challenge—even the best players in the world set up incorrectly from time to time.

The third major reason for mis-hit shots is a lack of trust. As I mentioned in the first chapter, when you lack trust, tension builds up in your swing, disrupting your rhythm, tempo, and synchronization, and often results in an off-line or mis-hit shot. This holds true for all shots, from drives to putts. Trusting your swing is crucial, but without a properly prepared mental approach to your game, trust can sometimes be as elusive as a sunny winter day in Seattle.

How the S.A.T. Process Got its Name

Recently, I conducted a workshop with the Carmel, California, High School boys' golf team. Many of the players were already familiar with the need for a pre-shot routine, but I saw some puzzled faces when I said that a post-shot routine is every bit as important, if not more so. I took some time and explained to my young audience that a successful post-shot routine performs a unique function, separate from, but similar in content to that of a pre-shot routine. We talked in detail about how the majority of mis-hit shots can be traced to a breakdown in *strategy, aim, or trust*. As I neared the end of my presentation, one of the young students looked at me with a big smile on his face. "I know what this is!" he exclaimed. "It's our S.A.T. test!" He was referring, of course, to the initials of the three elements, strategy, aim and trust. The boys were already familiar with the initials S.A.T., as in the Scholastic Aptitude Test, the required examination for entrance into many colleges.

I looked at assistant coach Curt Breitfuss, whose 'day job' is working as a hedge-fund manager and president of Tee Time (which sponsors aspiring professional golfers), and laughed. We thought it was a clever way to encapsulate the process, and the name stuck. It's more of a process than a test, though, so I modified it to the 'S.A.T. Process.'

How the Process Works

Although it is intensive, the S.A.T. Process usually takes less than five seconds to perform. The first step is to objectively evaluate the shot you just hit. It is critical for you to be nonjudgmental in this evaluation. Instead of saying, "What a jerk I am! I sliced it again!" you say something like, "Well, that shot went to the right."

After you've evaluated the shot you just hit, take a moment to clear your mind, and then take a swing, either literally or in your imaginative mind, with the feel, rhythm, and tempo that you want on your next swing. By doing this, you are replacing the feel of the errant swing with that of a proper one. This process prepares you both mentally and physically to make a strong, positive swing and begins to refocus you for the next shot.

The S.A.T. Process also calls for you to take a moment, after you've struck the ball correctly, to watch the beauty of the ball in flight and sense the joy of seeing it bouncing down the fairway or coming to rest near the pin. These moments are critically important because they allow you to indelibly stamp the image and feel of a good shot on your internal-feedback system, creating long-term memory and easy access to your recall process for the next shot. Would this attitude be different from the way you usually play?

Does it sound more enjoyable? It's a learned process, and you can do it. It might just change the way you feel about your game—and allow you to score better as well.

Each of you, of course, should put your own customized spin on this process, but nearly all of the players I've introduced to the S.A.T. Process—including professionals on several tours—love this tool and through it have experienced breakthrough improvements in their games. Players at all ability levels, including McCarron, have found the S.A.T. Process to be extremely beneficial.

"It's helped me tremendously," Scott said. "I really feel calm out there. If I hit a shot off-line, I quickly go through the process and then replace that shot in my mind with the feel I want. Yet, as important as it is to my game now, the S.A.T Process can be of even greater benefit to amateurs than it is to professionals. I think the S.A.T. Process is one of the best and easiest mental tools ever developed. If I sound enthusiastic about this process, it's because I am. I can't imagine ever again playing under pressure without utilizing it. The beauty of the S.A.T. Process is that it enables you to be immediately aware of the cause of a mis-hit shot, helps you get rid of anger and frustration, and lets you jettison all the emotional baggage that those negative emotions cause. It allows you to reconnect with your target and get ready for your next shot."

Jeff Brehaut, a PGA-TOUR professional from the San Francisco Bay Area, has also embraced the S.A.T. Process. "It's become a critical part of my game," said Jeff. "I go through it during every round on the Tour. I know I have to decide on a strategy, commit to it, get aimed physically and mentally to the target, trust my swing and then let it rip. When I mis-hit a shot, I know I didn't perform one or more of those steps. I feel the swing I intended to make and then go hit the next shot."

Nick Ushijima, the superlative Japanese, amateur player I introduced to you in the prior chapters, learned that the S.A.T.

Process allows him to evaluate shots in just the right way. "I've found I need to evaluate in a certain way so that I don't let myself get too involved in the technique process," Nick said. "I perform best when I am nonjudgmental and therefore less mechanically involved. Instead, I focus my attention on trusting my swing."

A Closer Look at *Strategy, Aim, and Trust*

Evaluating just why you mis-hit a shot is the most critical step in the process. Understanding the evaluation process also provides a keen insight into your game and into your mental state. I've found in my workshops that golfers of all skill levels enjoy learning more about it, and we often spend a great deal of time discussing it. Here is a closer look at the three primary elements of the evaluation process. Take note that there is a close relationship between the pre-shot and post- shot routines. You'll learn in upcoming chapters that the S.A.T. describes the organization of the pre-shot routine, too.

Strategy

It's instructive to think about how often we don't fully commit to our own strategies. We've all done it, often several times during a single round. Each shot we hit requires us to develop a separate strategy and to create an image of the shot itself. Maybe we want to hit a soft draw into a left-hand pin placement on a par three, or perhaps we decide to hit a three wood over a lake on a par five in hopes of getting to the green in two. But, sometime during our swing, our commitment to the shot fizzles like a wet firecracker. A gap appears between the strategy we chose and our belief that we can actually hit the shot. We bail out mentally. This, as most of you know, causes a flaw to appear that is usually characterized by hurried, jerky movements and a breakdown of the swing. It happens all the time. We fail to follow our own strategy because we never truly commit to it. Even a risky strategy carried out with full commitment and trust has a greater chance of succeeding than a conservative strategy without commitment.

In a recent round of golf at Incline Village with a group of friends (all early devotees to *Winning the Battle Within*), one of them, Larry Mitchell, hit a wonderful drive on the sixteenth hole and had only 110 yards to the pin. As he stood over his shot, I could actually see him tightening up. As result, his swing was full of tension and he shanked his pitching wedge out of bounds. His next shot was rhythmic and graceful, and he knocked it stiff to the pin. In a conversation on the next tee, Larry admitted he had approached the first shot with doubt in his mind as to whether or not he had enough club. He realized that he never resolved that conflict in his mind and therefore never committed to the club or the strategy he had chosen. As a result, he was not able to visualize or feel the shot in his imaginative mind, and he hurried his swing. If the story sounds familiar, it's because we've all done this on the golf course—failed to fully commit to our own strategies.

Properly using the S.A.T. Process helps us become much more aware of the need to design a clear strategy for each shot and then commit to that strategy. This is the first evaluative step in the S.AT. Process. Whenever you mis-hit a shot, your first thoughts should be: "Hmmm, I hit that off-line. Why? Did I fail to fully accept and commit to the strategy I chose for the shot?" By the way, be sure to complete this process on the spot. Don't wait until the next day to think about it.

Choosing the Right Strategy

I think you already know how long it takes to evaluate whether or not you committed to your pre-shot strategy—about a millisecond in most cases. If you're honest with yourself, you generally know even before the swing is completed. If you fully commit to your strategy and swing with trust, you're usually going to be happy with the result. On the other hand, if you don't believe in the shot or fully commit to your strategy, you'll probably be thinking about it while hunting for your ball in the tall grass.

Okay, but what does it really mean to commit to a shot? First, it means you have to consciously admit to yourself that there is a choice to be made—"I can hit the six iron or the seven iron." You should then ask, "Which shot is most comfortable for me? Which club produces positive feedback from my imaginative mind?"

You should develop your strategy for each shot and commit to it before you take your stance over the ball. Here is a critical tip— choose the shot that produces the best imagery and feel in your mind. Most often, if you allow your conscious mind—where you think about swing technique or how important the shot is—to over-ride your imaginative mind, it will be difficult for you to fully com-mit to your shot.

"When I'm playing well, I'm always in my imaginative mind," says McCarron. "I see and feel the shot in my mind before I hit it. I'm being totally creative out there. When I want to hit a low draw, for example, I don't get technical and swing step by step. I simply imagine the shot in my mind, and then I just do it. The body knows how to react. It will do what you are feeling. This works even if you are a higher handicapper. You'll be pleasantly surprised at how often you can hit a strategic shot, if you simply see it beforehand and resist thinking about the mechanics. It's amazing how often you'll hit quality shots, if you choose a comfortable strategy and then commit to it."

You should confirm your commitment during your pre-shot routine, as you are standing behind the ball ready to approach it and get into your stance. Often, it works best to consciously tell yourself, "Yes, I could hit a six, but I'm choosing to hit a firm seven iron, and I'm fully committed to that shot."

Another element of committing to your shot includes—as Scott mentioned—seeing and feeling the shot in your imaginative mind before you swing. See it, feel it, commit to it. It's amazing how powerful this is and how it can immediately enhance your game.

The same holds true for all your shots. For example, you may be facing a downhill, four-foot putt that appears to break two inches to the right. You set up over the ball and aim two inches to the left, but you begin to doubt that there is that much break. Instead of committing to your strategic line, you lose trust and fail to accelerate the putter head through the ball. As a result, the putt wobbles off line. As Bob Rotella says in his books and presentations, "A stroke starting from a committed strategy, even if slightly misread, has a much better chance of going in the hole than a stroke without commitment."

Committing to a strategy and seeing the shot in your imaginative mind go hand in hand. For example, you may be faced with a difficult lie and immediately the tension within you begins to build. You're angry over your bad luck and anxious about hitting the ball out of the bad lie. Addressing, acknowledging, and dealing with this potential toxic mix of anger and anxiety are essential parts of a successful commitment to a strategy.

You might say to yourself, "Okay, I got a bad break. So what? That happens to everybody. Now, I've got a chance to hit a really cool shot out of this divot. I'm going to relax for a minute and 'see' the ball coming out of the divot and landing on the green. Once I 'see' it, I can do it." It also helps tremendously if you have practiced for all contingencies (bad lies, etc.) on the practice range.

If you can't 'see' or 'feel' a successful shot, then try a different club selection or angle of attack until you find a shot that's comfortable for you. As Kirk Tripplett aptly describes, "Select a

conservative strategy and make an aggressive play." Tom
Kubistant, a Reno-based sport psychologist, recommends allowing
your swing to come from deep within rather than forcing a shot to
a risky target.

Take the Time it Takes

If you are concerned about the time it will take to perform your
S.A.T. Process, you need not worry. As I mentioned, it usually
takes less than five seconds. However, in order to allow this speedy
integration of psycho-physiological data to formulate in competition, I recommend that you practice your S.A.T. Process on the
range first. Whenever you mis-hit a shot on range, take a moment
and go through your S.A.T. Process. It's best to do this while conducting a contingency practice session, which is where you simulate, as closely as possible, the actual conditions and situations
involved in competitive play. We'll talk about contingency practice
in more depth later, but for now, it's important to realize that you
should practice conducting the S.A.T. Process just as you practice
your swing. This is especially important if you haven't conducted
a post-shot routine before. By practicing your S.A.T. Process,
you'll also be able to customize it to fit your game.

Shooting for Par

Getting back to the importance of buying into your own strategy,
I'm reminded of a story that one of my golf-professional colleagues, Bobby Siravo, told me recently. He was playing the
Northern California PGA at Winchester Country Club located just
east of Auburn, California. As he approached his tee shot on the
fifteenth hole, a treacherous peninsular par three, Siravo backed
off three times before finally playing his shot. He told me after-

THE S.A.T. PROCESS—FIVE SECONDS THAT WILL CHANGE YOUR GAME   69

ward that he worried about that tee shot the night before and during the round, knowing he could be in contention for the lead at that point. Of course, placing that much importance on one shot makes the shot very difficult indeed. Bobby told me he just couldn't commit to a cut 5 iron, thus the ball found the water to the right of the green.

"Given my mental state on the tee that day, what should I have done differently?" Bobby asked me. I suggested that because he could not commit to a shot at the pin, he should have changed his strategy and simply played a four iron to the back of the green, far away from the water. He would be faced with a long putt, but his chances for a par would have improved immensely. A shot like that also takes anything worse than a bogey out of the equation, and occasionally he might even make that long putt for a birdie. The fact is, though, sometimes you just have to shoot for a par. Bobby enjoyed five years of competitive golf on the mini tours and used all the lessons he learned to become a top-flight teacher, equipment storeowner, and club-fitter in northern California.

Committing to a club selection that fits your game, and to a target line that fits the situation, allow you to greatly reduce the tension in your swing so you can let the swing go. This permits you to move easily from your conscious mind to your imaginative mind so you can swing automatically and in rhythm.

Let's say you perform your S.A.T. Process after a mis-hit shot and you determine that you did not commit to your strategy. This evaluation is critical for two reasons. First, it prevents you from losing confidence in your swing. If you realize you didn't commit to your shot, then you know right away why your swing was flawed. It didn't break down for some obscure technical or mechanical reason. It broke down because of your lack of commitment. The remedy, then, is to take a rehearsal swing, fully committing to the shot this time in your mind. Get your rhythm back and 'see' the shot land where you want it to. What you are doing—and this is what Scott was referring to earlier—is replacing the 'feel' of a mis-hit shot with that of the one you wanted.

Your Technique is Rarely to Blame

It's an unfortunate fact that most players become instantly judgmental about their golf swings when shots go awry. They lose trust because they feel a mis-hit shot is caused by an imperfect technical swing, when in fact, it is a direct result of a failure to commit to the shot.

Perhaps the most important thing for golfers to realize is that many mis-hit shots do not result from technical flaws. They are the result of tension creeping into the body because of a lack of trust or commitment to a shot. *Doubt produces more missed shots than any other single cause!*

To sum up, when you mis-hit a shot, immediately check to see whether it was caused by doubts about your strategy. If it was, replace your swing feel and then make a mental note to more fully commit to your strategy on your next shot.

Aim

The second common reason for mis-hit shots is incorrect aim or misalignment. PGA-TOUR players say this is a recurring problem for players on the Tour—the misaligning of feet, hips, or shoulders to the target line. Aiming or aligning your body correctly to the target is essential to striking the ball well.

This is the only part of the book where I address a technical aspect of executing the swing. Aiming correctly is essential to hitting consistent, quality shots. I've always thought of aiming in golf as analogous to the alignment of a missile on a launching pad. If the missile is misaligned by just a few inches, it may miss its target by miles once it is in space.

Incorrect alignment in golf may not cause you to blow up the wrong planet, of course, but the mis-hit shots that result might just send you into emotional orbit now and then. You should pay close attention to your alignment before every shot. At the end of the round, we want you to report, "Houston, we have no problems. We are right on target."

Aim is critical in everything from launching big drives to stroking three-foot putts. The frame of reference that most enlightened teachers use when they talk about aim is to get the player's hips, shoulders, and heels aligned parallel left of the target. This is what we call an athletically 'square' alignment. Some teachers and a few players intentionally open or close their alignments from square, but it is the place from which they all start.

The clubface should aim directly at the target in a square alignment. Some players prefer to slightly open the clubface, but again, all adjustments begin from the square position.

There is a second element in aiming, and it is equally important to understanding the square position. That element is aiming the ball flight and your body in your imagination. It's what I call getting the energy out in front of you. Successful players do this in variety of ways. Some people see the entire shot and flight of the ball; others simply see the target in their minds, like a great free-throw shooter sees the front or back of the rim. Some see only the trajectory of the shot. I've had players tell me they see the arc of the shot in color when they are playing well. Others see only the end of the shot, as the ball hits the green and spins back to the hole. As a rule, the closer you get to the green, the more vivid these images become. How many times have you nailed a putt dead center after seeing the ball go into the hole in your imaginative mind? I've also had players tell me they don't see the shot at all—rather they feel it. The important thing is that you should see or feel something aligned to the target in your imaginative mind that matches your physical alignment.

These two things work directly together. As a rule of thumb, if you aren't comfortable with your physical alignment, it's going to be very difficult to picture a successful shot in your imaginative mind. That's a good time to back away from the shot, regroup, re-aim, and then trust your swing.

Trust

When you lack trust, tension builds up in your swing, which usually translates into a less-than-desirable shot. By the way, this holds true for all shots, including putts.

Trusting your swing is crucial, as McCarron points out: "I would say lack of trust is the number one reason PGA-TOUR players mis-hit shots. A missed shot is usually the result of a negative thought or doubt of some type creeping into the player's mind during or before the swing. The problem is that the golf industry as a whole would have us believe that all bad shots are the result of bad mechanics. Golfers are bombarded every day with technical advice about their golf swings. What's the first thing that happens when a player hits a bad shot during or before a tournament on television? The guys in the booth get out the telestrator, analyze where the swing got off plane, and give some highly technical reason why this happened. Although the analysis may be accurate in terms of how the swing broke down, it is incorrect as to why it broke down. I'll guarantee you that the vast majority of the time the swing broke down because the player didn't trust it. Most likely, he held onto the swing too long because he didn't trust his strategy or he never saw the shot in his imaginative mind. Most of the time there isn't anything wrong with the player's swing—it's just that he didn't trust it on that one shot. I'd love to hear a television analyst say that, because if you ask almost any professional golfer, they'll tell you how critical trust and commitment are to any shot."

Evaluate, Don't Judge

Remember, during your evaluation process, take care not to judge your shot harshly. In *Extraordinary Golf,* author Fred Shoemaker describes the first few seconds after hitting a shot as the crucial time for emotional and imaginative awareness to emerge. Judging a shot stifles awareness, and access to information that can help future shots is lost.

Harsh judgment has no place in the S.A.T. Process. Mistakes must be seen as investments in progress. If you missed the shot because your tempo was too fast, evaluate it, and then replace it with a rhythmic swing and a proper tempo.

Being judgmental about your swing or your shot will inevitably lead to a long day. Frankly, only a small percentage of golfers are *not* judgmental, and that is one reason average handicaps across the country have failed to drop in recent years, in spite of the great advances in the quality of equipment and teaching resources.

The next time you tee it up, commit to concentrating throughout the entire round on not being judgmental of your shots. If you replace judgment with the S.A.T. Process, I think you'll be surprised at how much better you'll play and how much more fun the game will be.

I know that being nonjudgmental is a hard thing to do. Most players have been self-critical for so long that it takes a sustained effort to break the habit. Being judgmental is deeply embedded in golf culture. But, remember, it's only a habit. You can train yourself to be nonjudgmental, but it will take discipline. Once it becomes habitual, though, you'll have more fun playing and your scores will improve. You'll also become more aware of how often your fellow players harshly judge their own shots and how often that leads to yet another poor shot.

The top players in the world clearly know the importance of this nonjudgmental approach. Have you ever heard Tiger Woods, after a round, harshly judge himself or his golf shots? Frankly, I've never heard him do that, and I think that is one of the primary reasons for his success. At times, Tiger does respond with anger over mis-hit shots, and I know he would be better served if he did not. But, to Tiger's credit, the anger seldom lasts more than a few moments. Moreover, I've never heard Annika Sorenstam, Phil Mickelson, Ernie Els, Julie Inkster, or Vijay Singh talk poorly about their golf shots. You may think that's because they don't hit any poor shots, but on a relative scale, compared to other professionals, they all mis-hit shots from time to time. The difference is they don't think of them as poor shots, but rather as opportunities to learn and gain corrections for their next shot. They know that harsh self-judgment yields no valuable or constructive information.

Taking Responsibility for Every Shot

Maintaining a nonjudgmental attitude is related directly to another critical aspect of your mental approach—taking responsibility for every shot you make. We'll talk about storytelling, self-talk, and something psychologists like to call 'cognitive restructuring' later on, but it's important right now to understand that by being non-judgmental about your game and each individual shot, it becomes much easier to take responsibility for each shot. In golf, there are no pinch hitters, relief pitchers, or substitute players—it's just you out there hitting every shot on your own. Once you buy in to the idea that you are responsible for every shot you hit, the game actually becomes easier. You can spend a great deal of time and effort explaining why a shot went awry, when it is so much simpler and more constructive to analyze, in a nonjudgmental way, why the ball flew the way it did, and then apply the necessary corrective measures so it doesn't happen again.

The S.A.T. Process Summary

Here is a step-by-step look at how to conduct your own S.A.T. Process.

1. Review—Objectively Evaluate. Directly following a mishit shot, take a moment and ask yourself what caused the shot to be less-than-desirable. Was it strategy, aim, lack of trust, or a combination thereof? Remember, make no judgments; just do a quick evaluation.

2. Rehearse—Correct the Problem. Once you've determined which of these, or combination thereof, caused the errant shot, then set up and take a rehearsal swing, correcting the problem.

3. Replace—Gain a Positive Feel. Immerse yourself in your imaginative mind and record how the correct swing should feel. This immediately erases the negative thoughts and feelings from the shot you just mis-hit and replaces them with elements of trust and rhythm. Let the feel of the rehearsed shot replace the one you just hit, and then head for your next shot with a confident stride.

I want to include a helpful tip before we roll into the next chapter. While the S.A.T. Process is straightforward and easy to understand, you may find yourself applying it inconsistently at first. The one thing required to make it work is patience, and we all tend to lose patience when we mis-hit shots. Try a couple of rounds just focusing on the S.A.T. Process, so it becomes an automatic part of your game. Remember, you should also use the S.A.T.

process when you hit a good shot, but in a slightly different way. Just stand back and allow your internal-feedback system to admire and record your graceful, powerful swing and the solid contact you just made. Be aware that you need to consciously make the S.A.T. Process a habit at first. But, once you make it a part of your game, it will come automatically, and you will see steady improvement in your score and in your enjoyment of the round.

7

THE CIRCLE OF PERFORMANCE AND GOAL SETTING

Another critical key to a positive and healthy mental game is to become balanced in our approach to performance. Balance, of course, is important in all aspects of our lives. Aristotle wrote that the pathway to happiness is to seek the "mean between the extremes." I don't know if Aristotle ever teed it up with his friends on some ancient Grecian golf course, but if he did, I'm sure he would have been a single-digit handicapper. With Aristotle's premise in mind, let's examine the elements of the Circle of Performance, how they can be kept in balance, and how they interact with impact performance.

The Circle of Performance is a comprehensive performance package that includes 12 elements that have been distilled through years of *Winning-the-Battle-Within* experiences and consultations with numerous golfers of all skill levels. Here are the 12 elements:

1. Philosophy (values, integrity, beliefs);
2. Instruction;
3. Golf Technique;

 4. Nutrition;
 5. Physical Conditioning;
 6. Relationships;
 7. Organization of Work or School;
 8. Equipment and Club-fitting;
 9. Recovery;
10. Quality practice;
11. Inner Game; and
12. Mental Game.

To win the battle within, each of these elements must receive attention and be kept in balance with the others. The players who attend my seminars usually look forward to this part of the workshop. It's a time for inner reflection, exploration, and learning. This is done in a nonjudgmental way, and most players really enjoy the journey. Each of these elements is critical to top sport performance. If even one is neglected, it can throw off the overall balance. After each element has been described and evaluated—this usually takes about an hour—the inner game, quality practice, and the mental game are emphasized. These are the central thrust of applied sport psychology, the workshop, and the *Winning-the-Battle-Within* belief system for performance.

One of the challenges golfers face is that the commercial golfing culture tends to ignore many of these elements in favor of a few. For example, equipment fitting and quality instruction are the only two that you usually see on television or read about in golf magazines because they produce the revenue streams for the golf industry. Don't get me wrong, I believe in our economic system, and I certainly value quality instruction and correct equipment. In this case, however, the mental and physical balance we need is often obscured by the constant attention focused on the most recent titanium driver and the latest Tiger Woods swing change. Contrary to Aristotle's thesis, this is an example of the extreme and not the mean.

The Pie—'Slice by Slice'

Fellow applied sport psychologist, Neale Smith, calls the Circle of Performance a 'pie' and concurs that each slice of the pie is a separate element. After earning his Master's Degree in Sport Psychology with Ken Ravizza at California State University, Fullerton, Neale became a professional golfer in 1992. At the end of his first year of play, he won the PGA qualifying tournament, a remarkable feat. A series of back injuries forced him to leave the

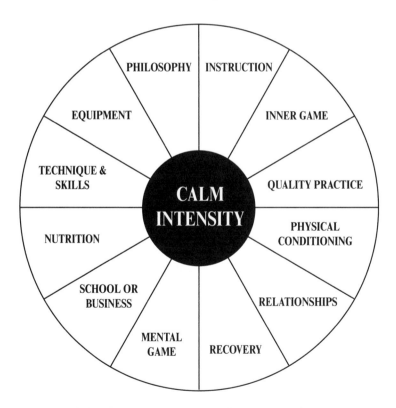

CIRCLE OF PERFORMANCE

PGA TOUR, but the Tour's loss has become many a player's gain, because he is now utilizing his sport psychology skills for golfers.

As I would at the start of a *Winning-the-Battle-Within* workshop, I am going to describe these elements slice by slice. Remember, the slices are not independent variables, but rather dependent upon one another for optimum performance. Slices are dynamically larger or smaller, depending upon which you want to maximize and improve.

What I'd like you to do right now is give some thought to each element and how it applies to you and your performance. The exercise will help reveal how balanced you are. By going through the Circle of Performance, you'll learn what areas may need more of your attention than others. If you want, you can give each slice an evaluative number, of say, from one to ten, with ten being the highest score and one the lowest. For example, you might feel exceptionally confident that you are getting top-notch instruction from a teacher who knows how technical instruction should blend into your psychological and body makeup. You might feel confident that the pro is focused on getting you to develop a swing you can trust rather than giving you different swing thoughts each time you take a lesson. If this is the case, you may want to give your enlightened teacher a ten. At the same time, you may have fallen off the wagon in terms of your diet and conditioning regime. It may be that you're beginning to look more like the Michelin Man than you'd care to admit. You may want to give yourself a five or so, while vowing to get back to the gym.

In addition to the workshop evaluations, I work with top professionals and amateurs to develop specific evaluations of their games also based on the Circle of Performance. It's an instructive exercise for most of the players, and they usually find it extremely important to the overall understanding of their games. I'm going to briefly explain here how it's done, and combine it with the work-shop evaluations so you can evaluate your own game the way the pros do, if you'd like.

Evaluating Your Own Circle of Performance

I like to begin an analysis of the performance circle with an examination of a player's philosophy. Answering the question, "Why do you play golf?" reveals dominant motivations that provide a valuable foundation for setting your performance goals and evaluating your overall play. They also reveal much about your mental approach to the game. Generally, these answers fall into two categories—external and internal. External motivations include fame, fortune, and recognition, while internal motivations include statements like "I love playing golf. I can hardly wait to practice. There is no greater joy then playing a round of golf with my friends. I love competition. Every time I play, I learn more about my game and myself."

Because external forces come and go (fame can be ever-fleeting), it is dangerous to allow them to be your dominant motivation. If a player finds that the desired fame remains elusive, motivation to stay on the performance path decreases. The highest-octane fuel for motivation—the passion that drives us to train and compete—resides inside us. My experience with players across all skill levels is that internal motivation is the driving force that lasts for a lifetime. Reaching for the highest rung on the ladder of performance serves you well, but reaching inward for internal balance and internal satisfaction will serve you better.

The philosophical discussions ("Why do you play golf?") are lively and revealing. They provide an excellent starting point for evaluations of the remaining slices of the pie.

Quality of Your Swing Lessons

You can evaluate this slice of the pie by asking whether, after your last lesson with a professional, you felt you truly improved. There are times when you might feel just the opposite and remain frustrated for weeks. Don't blame yourself if this happens. Changes can take time, but if the frustration continues after you have given them the appropriate practice attention, you should reevaluate your relationship with your instructor. You might consider another teacher with a different approach. It is not always the content of the lesson that may not be working. It could be communication, teaching philosophy, accessibility, or other factors in the complex, teacher-student relationship.

I encourage all of my students, pros and amateurs alike, to research the teaching skill and reputation of available golf professionals. Ask other players whose opinions you trust, check out periodicals, observe teachers in action, and then interview two to three teachers to determine the best fit for your goals and personality.

Golf Technique Goals

Determining what you want to achieve in the upcoming season with regard to swing improvements requires you to evaluate your own game and your work with your swing coach. What do you both think of your swing? Remember, neither of you should be judgmental here—just evaluate, as objectively as possible, how well you think you swing the club. Chances are you swing it better than you think you do.

When evaluating this slice of the pie, ask yourself what you want to achieve this year in terms of understanding your swing. It's helpful to make a list. You might want to concentrate on better alignment, a fuller turn, a different swing plane, or perhaps you want to learn how to trust your swing more fully. Whatever technique you choose, stick to a long-range practice plan. Remember, there are no shortcuts to improved play. After quality practice the new technique will find a place in your long-term memory and allow automatic play eventually to kick-in.

Nutrition

The need for good nutrition speaks for itself, yet for men especially, its voice is rarely heard. It may come as a shock to some, but beer, burgers, and fries do not make a meal for champions. Nearly all the players on the tours these days pay at least some attention to nutrition. Choose a diet as wisely as you choose your swing coach, club fitter, or sport psychologist. Many top players have become quite serious about nutrition. I've had great talks with players like Robert Hamilton, who shuns caffeine-containing soft drinks while traveling on the Canadian Tour. He also insists on cooking much of his own food, even while traveling between tournaments.

"I stay away from fast-food as much as I can," said Robert, who looks fit enough to run a marathon. "A big way to avoid sugar and too much saturated fat is to bring your own nutritional snacks to the course with you. Otherwise, you get hungry out there and you naturally grab a candy bar or something else that isn't good for you. You may have to make up your own snacks, but most of us can squeeze out five minutes to do this. I find it makes me feel better knowing I'm doing everything I can to make myself competitive."

It is not a bad investment of time to bring yourself up to speed on meals and nutritional snacks designed to maintain energy and blood-sugar levels.

Strength and Conditioning

Physical conditioning is closely related to nutrition. You don't have to go gonzo and run four-minute miles or play 48-minute basketball games to be in shape, but you should make exercise a regular part of your life. Remember to toss in some flexibility exercises while you are at it. If you have health problems, check with your physician, and then put together a physical-fitness program with the help of a physical therapist or conditioning coach who understands the biomechanics of a golf swing. The PGA TOUR's physical-fitness mobile van is well known by now. The players today are bigger, stronger, and more physically fit than ever. Stretching and flexibility are critical components of the huge drives players hit these days. Tiger, Ernie, Vijay, and Sergio are all fitness buffs. Although there are no fitness vans traveling with the mini-tours, numerous players I know are finding creative ways to maintain fitness.

I have learned a great deal about physical therapy and conditioning for golf from well-trained physical therapists and conditioning coaches like Todd Eeckhoff, who has been working with McCarron for years. Working out of the Reno Orthopedic Group, Todd has developed a useful combination-therapy-and-conditioning program specific to golf performance. If you haven't worked out in a while, it won't be long (especially if you work with someone like Todd) before you remember how rewarding it can be. McCarron is not a physical giant, but he remains one of the longer hitters on the PGA TOUR. He credits his length off the tee to the hard work he has put in to become one of the most flexible players on Tour.

"I think conditioning is critical," Scott told me. "All the pros know that these days, and I think amateurs' games would improve tremendously if they worked on flexibility and conditioning. It's important for your mind and your body." Triplett thinks that his work with Roger Craig, a Scottsdale conditioning coach who for over two decades has worked with numerous elite athletes in all sports, and a recent change in diet have added considerably to the longevity of his career.

Relationships

Perhaps as important as any element on the chart is the quality of your relationships. This begins, of course, with your core relationships, which may include your spouse, partner, parents, friends, and whatever spiritual entity you happen to believe in. Sometimes it's not easy for us to delve into the quality of these relationships, but it is a healthful thing to do from time to time. They are the foundations of our lives. If they are not right, it can be difficult to achieve the mental attitude necessary for peak performances. In an enlightening passage in *Golf in the Kingdom,* Murphy found that he was having difficulty lining up his putts. As soon as he made a major philosophical change at the Esalen Institute (he is its co-founder and CEO), he found the change not only helped him discover the true line in his putting, it helped line up his life in some significant ways.

A great part of the long-term success enjoyed by McCarron and Triplett on the PGA TOUR has come because both of them highly value their core relationships with their supportive, aware, and perceptive wives, Jennifer and Cathi, their families, and their friends. Their home lives are positive and productive, full of love, compassion, and caring for the people around them. Sure, I know that many successful athletes are ego-centric and self-absorbed, but I do not consider them so successful or fulfilled as human beings as players like Scott and Kirk. Their successes go much deeper than those of self-centered athletes who are so apt, these days, to have narrow belief systems with little awareness of the world outside of themselves and their respective sports. I caution you not to overlook this essential part of your life.

Organization of Work or School

Another important element of our lives that's easy to overlook is our emotional attitude toward and attention given to our jobs or to our schoolwork. These are core attitudes that, if left unattended, can affect our inner mental balance and rob us of patience or trust. A good attitude leads directly to quality organization of our tasks. Balance occurs naturally, and a quiet efficiency takes over the mind.

Most of us are aware of how difficult it is to play golf when we are preoccupied with something unfinished or unpleasant at work or at school. It's almost impossible to prepare for or play a good round of golf when we are fighting with a supervisor; getting a D in chemistry, scrambling to finish a work project, or struggling to complete a practice schedule. Conversely, when things are going well at work, golf can become an easy game. More often than not, our emotional state, centered on the quality of our work or participation at school, dictates our success on the golf course. Evaluated correctly, a golf round can be a wonderful barometer that reveals our emotional state of mind.

I have found it to be essential for tour players, or amateurs seeking elite status, to have well-organized practice and playing schedules. Scheduling can be complex for all golfers, from professions without fully exempt status on a tour, or with limited funds, to the busy amateur, who has a job and a family. I recommend that amateurs, especially, view their golf rounds and practice time as the 'reward' they give themselves for all the hard work they put in at their jobs. Part of being successful in this slice of the Circle of Performance is learning to play golf 'guilt-free.' Remember, you deserve time to follow your passions.

Equipment and Club-fitting

Golf equipment gets better every year. Be sure to be fitted by a professional when you buy new clubs and ask for a recommendation of the type of ball that fits your game as well. Make sure you tell the club fitter that you are not there to buy clubs, but rather to buy club-fitting expertise. But, remember, the club doesn't execute the swing—you do. Ultimately, you are far more important to the outcome of your golf game than the equipment you use.

It's imperative that all career professionals take full advantage of the advanced technology for club fitting that is available. An incredibly potent combination of shaft components, club-head configurations, ball flight, and spin can be identified at the technology centers like Bobby Siravo's Golf Etc in Folsom, California, or the Nakashima Center in Stockton, California.

Recovery

Recovery has different meanings, depending on how serious you are about your golf. For professionals, the recovery time that is most important is the time it takes to revitalize the emotional and physical energy required to compete in an intense environment week after week. For amateurs, recovery can have a different meaning—as in how long it takes to decompress from the stresses of job, school, or relationships in order to relax and play an enjoyable round.

To the touring professionals, I always pose the question, "How effective are you in scheduling productive time away from your tour?" Recovery from emotional fatigue usually includes time away from golf, time with an outside business, time with family and friends, and traveling. McCarron used his last time home to increase the intensity and duration of his workouts. I refer to what Scott did as 'active recovery.' Triplett uses time away to 'empty out the mental garbage' that has accumulated during the year's schedule. Amateurs must do something similar before teeing it up, but the 'mental garbage' usually involves daily stresses outside the realm of golf. For professionals, developing an effective recovery routine is critical to long-term success because professional golf can be an extremely taxing. For amateurs, learning how to relax and shut out the rest of the world and have fun on the course are paramount to enjoying the game and playing well.

Quality Practice

Quality practice is a must, if you want to reach a sustained level of peak performance. Think about the times that you practice. Do you walk away from the practice tee with a sense of accomplishment, or do you leave confused and less trusting than when you arrived? Do you feel you have a solid practice routine, or do you, like most golfers, grab a bucket of balls and try to repeat the same swing over and over with the same club? How much time can you spend practicing? Regardless of the amount, you should resolve to spend it as wisely as possible. You should customize your practice regimen to fit your game. For example, if you play 90 percent of your golf on a narrow course with wide, flat greens, you may want to concentrate your practice on hitting shots that will get you into play off the tee. If the course is wide open with tough, undulating greens, you may decide to concentrate on iron play, chipping, and putting. Ideally, you should find a balance among simulated, technical, and trust practice routines as well as between the short game and the long. I'll talk more about quality practice in later chapters and provide some tips on how to turn your practice sessions into tens.

Mental Game

Evaluating your mental game means reviewing the quality of your positive self-talk, self-confidence, mental toughness, attitude, posture, and motivation. In this slice of the pie, you should check to see whether or not you are taking full responsibility for all of your shots. At the same time, think about whether you are suspending judgment about errant shots or whether you are judging yourself too harshly. As I've pointed out, if you are nonjudgmental, you will initiate a faster and more efficient process to refocus for the next shot. This is also a great time to evaluate your pre-shot, in-between-shot, and post-shot routines and to determine whether you use them regularly in your practice sessions.

Inner Game

Here you should evaluate how consistently you see and feel your shots before you hit them. Is your internal feedback system operating effectively? Can you consistently trust your swing and stroke? Evaluating and subsequently developing your inner game is the most direct route to automatic play, which allows you to get 'in the zone' and stay in it. Be sure to complete the Awareness Questionnaire in the Appendix and evaluate your answers.

At the core of the Circle of Performance is calm intensity, an energy fuel that feeds into each category. It is a state of being that partners with self-confidence, compassion, attitude, intrinsic motivation, self-talk, and the management of emotions. It is the energy force as a player engages in training, competition, relationships, conditioning, etc.

The Quest for Balance

Balance in your golf swing and in all aspects of your life, is necessary to achieve consistent peak performances. Using the Circle of Performance is one of the best ways to remind yourself of all the elements of this overall balance. It is a good checklist to review from time to time, especially when your game is a little off and you find yourself losing patience on the golf course. A quick look at the Circle of Performance will usually reveal which of those elements may have become unbalanced in your life. Remember, too, that *Winning the Battle Within* gains its strength from the inner game, the mental game, and quality practice, the brightest stars in the Circle's galaxy.

Your Golf Goals in The Circle of Performance

Once a player becomes well versed in a personal philosophy during our workshops and has checked in on all the circle's elements, goal setting can begin in earnest. Goal setting guidelines are available in a short form for workshops and in a longer version for professionals. Both versions give considerable attention to action plans and methods of accountability. (See Appendix.)

The goals' evaluation usually is in two parts. First, players review the past year and determine whether they met or exceeded the goals they set for themselves at the end of the previous year. In working with top players such as McCarron, Wi and Triplett, for example, I found that they don't achieve all the goals they've set for themselves, because they set some of their goals quite high. Any series of goals should be a blend of 'reachable' and 'dream' goals. You should never set your goals so high as to attain none of them, but at the same time, a professional golfer should not set breaking 80 as a primary goal. For example, there have been years when Scott won more than a million dollars on the PGA TOUR (a pretty fine goal for most of us), but didn't reach his goal of making the Ryder Cup Team. In 2004, Scott didn't get the win he was looking for, but he made significant improvement in his driving accuracy and greens-in-regulation statistics. In 2005, Scott started fast, but tailed off the last half of the season. After reviewing 2005, plans for 2006 called for a renewal of passion, an increase in practice intensity and time, and the resolution of minor equipment issues.

Kirk also achieved some of his goals in 2004 and did not achieve others, which is always the case when there's a good blend of meaningful goals. Although he got off to a slow start, he finished the year near the top in driving accuracy, greens in regulation, and in one scoring category—accuracy from within one hundred yards of the flag. In July of 2005, elbow surgery cut short Kirk's season, but served as an unexpected extended and fruitful recovery period. His energy is at its highest moving forward into 2006.

More injuries to Kirk in 2008, and to Scott in 2007, caused both players to go through an entire new goal-setting process.

In 2002, Jeff Brehaut and I were discussing his goals for the year. He reflected upon the ineffectiveness of his goal-setting process. Jeff always set his goals early in the year, but if he didn't make much progress toward reaching them, he quickly abandoned them. Two things are wrong with that goal-setting strategy. First, goals are important, but when the emphasis is placed only upon achieving outcomes, players quickly lose interest when the goals are not immediately achieved. That was the case with Jeff. Second, goals are only effective when the player develops action plans to achieve them. Jeff hadn't added this necessary ingredient. This is a critical step for all of us. Don't forget, when you set goals for yourself, also ask what you will do on a consistent basis to give yourself an opportunity to reach them.

As a result of our conversation, Jeff loaded his goal-setting workbook with action plans covering the elements in the Circle of Performance. I also reminded Jeff that goals are not etched in stone. If the goals appear to be too high, or if they are reached before the year ends, they can be reset.

Jeff and I learned another lesson that year. In 2004, we decided to stretch his goals beyond, "I would like to retain my card." Setting goals like making the cut and keeping a PGA-TOUR card have a way of just missing. As a result, we changed his goals. One of his goals was to shoot for the top 70 on the money-earning list on the Tour. We also asked, "Why not play to be in contention to win every week?" We set a number of ambitious goals like these and even some dream goals.

Because goals that stretch one's limits are tied to the complexity of self-confidence, self-acceptance, and one's belief system, Jeff had to move out a bit. He had to accept in his mind that he is an excellent player. He had to reach into his deep beliefs and determine that, without equivocation, he belonged on the PGA TOUR. He put some hard work into this process and saw some nice results. He not only won the PGA's tortuous 'Q' School qualifying tournament, he finished in the top 90 in money earnings in 2003 and the top 60 in 2005. By elevating his goals, and designing an action plan to achieve them, he made significant strides as a player.

In August 2005, having reached one of his goals for the year—securing his PGA-TOUR card for 2006—Jeff was ready to reach higher. With a sense of urgency and a confident outlook, he set making the top 40 on the PGA-TOUR Money List as his new goal. Achieving this secures an automatic invitation to the Masters, which has been one of Jeff's life-long dreams. Getting to the Masters, albeit sweet, is not the main story, though; rather, it's the disciplined process Jeff adhered to that gets the prize and is fundamental to the *Winning-the-Battle-Within* approach to performance.

Updating Your Goals in the Circle of Performance

The second part of goal evaluation is to set new goals for the upcoming year. This should be done with deliberation. Part of the benefit of this exercise is to get you to visualize your success in the year ahead. You should 'see' yourself making improvements, whether it is shooting your best score ever, playing well in the club championship, breaking 100 for the first time, or getting out to the golf course once a week. Whatever it is, set goals that logically fit your game and the amount of time you can realistically spend on it. A well-organized set of goals, action plans, and a system for accountability for each category of the Circle of Performance are essential for continued performance improvement. It is also important to remember that it isn't only the attainment of the goals, but also the dogged pursuit of them that leads to positive self-growth and shapes one's character. You may have to revise your plan as things unfold, but start with a plan and you will achieve great results.

Goal setting is recognized as one of the strongest forces for personal motivation because it mobilizes energy and effort. They are specific targets to shoot for. Without goals, you are like a ship without a rudder, drifting along in no particular direction. It is important that you commit to your goals. Take ownership! The more you visualize and feel your goals, the more you kindle desire and gain inspiration for even greater effort.

The next time you rush out to the driving range, get a small bucket of balls instead of a large one, and spend the extra half hour you would otherwise have spent beating balls in planning, scheduling, or goal setting. The Circle of Performance, with its balanced approach, is a fun and powerful tool. You can use it in its entirety or refer back to specific slices of the pie as you go.

8

YOU CAN CHOOSE TO
BE CONFIDENT!

In the fall of 1993, a young player from Northern California sharpened his game and headed for 'Q' School in an attempt to follow his dream of making the PGA TOUR. The player was Scott McCarron, and as we discussed earlier in this book, he fell short of his dream that year.

Scott came back from that first stage of the qualifying feeling defeated. Later that very afternoon, Joey Ferrari, another fine golfer from northern California and a friend of both mine and Scott's, called me, said Scott wanted to strengthen his mental game, and asked if I would help. I liked Scott immediately. We met at my house and relaxed with a couple of cold beverages while we talked for a long time about the inner game of golf. It was a rich and enjoyable conversation that neither of us has forgotten.

"It was the first time I had ever heard anyone say that confidence is a matter of choice," Scott said later. "My mind was opened to new possibilities that afternoon, as we talked about things that have since become cornerstones of my success on the Tour. We all have dramatic and special turning points in our lives, and that afternoon was one of those for me."

Confidence is Not Dependent on Past Performance

One of the first things Scott and I talked about that day was the misconception that confidence is directly related only to the outcome of a previous performance. As it turned out, while we were talking, the San Francisco 49ers football team was playing on television. The sound was turned down low, but during a brief quiet time in our conversation, we heard the game announcer say, "Because 49ers quarterback, Steve Young, just completed his fourth pass in a row, his confidence is soaring."

"There!" I said, pointing at the television. "That's what's wrong! That's why people don't understand that every player on the field has control over whether to be confident regardless of past performances! These announcers have it backwards. Confidence is not a result of playing well; playing well is a result of being confident." (For more on this topic, read Bob Rotella's fine book, *Golf is a Game of Confidence.*)

The point I wanted to make to Scott was that waiting to become confident until you play well might mean that the round or the tournament could be over before you've allowed confidence to set in.

"Look," I continued, "confidence can be a matter of choice when it is not related to the outcome of your latest performance. Think of it this way. Consider separating the definition of confidence into external and internal confidence. External confidence is the type we always hear about. It's always based on the quality of an athlete's immediate past performances. In golf, that would translate to the last shot or two that you just hit. External confidence, however, is extremely fleeting and almost impossible to control, yet that's the type they always discuss on television, with Steve Young and just about every other athlete.

"The more enduring confidence is internal," I told Scott. "As an athlete or performer, you can gain control over your internal confidence. It is developed systematically through practicing properly, projecting positive imagery, clearing your mind of mechanical-swing thoughts, using positive self-talk, believing in your instructors, having a positive attitude, maintaining great posture, and most of all, increasing your trust."

Seeking the Infinite Wisdom

I waited a moment to allow what I'd said to sink in. Scott seemed fascinated by the concept of being able to control his own confidence levels, and he wanted to know more.

"Here is a powerful reality that nobody talks about on television," I said. "Internal confidence can be an acquired psychological state. You don't need a perfect technical swing or to have hit your previous shot perfectly to feel confident about your next one. Internal confidence begins with the unwavering belief that your mental and physical game fundamentals are correct and that you have practiced them properly. Confidence grows when you realize that the swing you have today is the one you will play with today and when you firmly resolve to trust it. It is strengthened by a non-judgmental approach to your game and by positive self-talk. Positive imagery follows positive self-talk and together they allow you to play in your imaginative mind. This sequence is critical to internal confidence and corresponding, high-performance golf rounds. Your confidence will continue to grow as you learn to be your own best friend. The self-talk, compassion, consideration, support, and empathy that you routinely extend to your best ball partner are, when directed to yourself, the foundation of internal self- confidence."

Now I was on a roll.

"Trust comes next, like the infinite wisdom of body and mind working in total harmony. Thelonious Monk plays incredible improvisational jazz, because he trusts himself and his music. Great golfers have the same trust. Teddy Roosevelt called it "the poem of a good athlete." Arnold Palmer, whose game was as charismatic and as improvisational as that of any golfer who ever walked onto a golf course, once said, "What other people find in poetry or art museums, I find in the flight of a good drive."

"What all this means," I concluded, "is that being confident about a particular shot has nothing at all to do with how superbly or how poorly you hit the previous shot. It is a state of mind that you can learn to put yourself into by practicing the things we've talked about. Once you get to this critical point, you will be amazed at how much more you will feel in control of your game, and when that happens, progress in unlimited."

The self-confidence they are talking about is really an athlete's sensory system remembering the 'feel' of well-timed shot. Together, the memory of the swing and the self-confident state have unmistaken power. Separately, I'll take internal self-confidence every time.

At this time, Scott took internal self-confidence into his belief system and took off in speedy pursuit of his PGA-TOUR career.

Developing Internal Confidence

The rest of this chapter is devoted to showing you how to develop and manage the critical components that must come together so you can build a solid foundation of internal confidence that will lead you toward the winner's circle. You'll find tips on how to handle fear, avoid storytelling, gain mental toughness, and change and restructure deep beliefs. The goal is to convince you that confidence is a matter of choice and that, through efficient practice, internal confidence can become a permanent part of your game and lifestyle.

Handling Fear

Even the great players confront their fears at some point in almost every meaningful round. As Lee Trevino so aptly put it, "Every golfer leaks a little oil once in a while."

For many players, however, fear can be an overwhelming and totally destructive force. Fear can manifest itself in a variety of forms, including the most obvious—the white-knuckled, stomach-clenching tension that, if left unaddressed, usually causes an out-of-sync swing. Yet, apathy, too, is a common way we deal with fear. We may think that apathy is the opposite of fear, but it is not. It is both a form of fear and a result of it. Apathy robs us of motivation, but it also has a narcotic effect—it takes away the pain. If we don't care, we don't fear, and we don't suffer. Apathy is a cleverly cloaked manifestation of fear. It causes carelessness and a lack of focus. Between white-knuckled tension and apathy are a number of other results of fear, including anger, frustration, anxiety, self-doubt, self-pity, excuse-making, resignation, and even excessive light-heartedness, which is just a step away from apathy. Fear has many colors, and none of them looks good on a scorecard. Unlike most other athletes, golfers must face fear for up to five hours a day for four or more days in a row. What follows are ways in which we can arm ourselves against our own fears and use the energy contained in that emotion to positive ends. Remember, merely stating and facing your fears is itself a confidence booster. You've taken the first step.

Capturing Fear's Energy

How do we handle fear? Can we destroy it and make it go away forever without becoming nervous or apathetic? The answer, unfortunately, is no. But, the truth is, we really don't want to totally vanquish fear, because its energy, when channeled to a positive emotion like dynamic energy, often provides the edge we need to play at our peak. Fear, if it is managed correctly, adds great vigor to our game. Fear's energy is like rocket fuel—it can send us to great heights, or it can explode on the launching pad. To gain confidence and become peak performers, we must learn how to harness the power of fear and use it to our own benefit.

One of the first things I do in my workshops is ask the players to address their fears directly. As Murphy wrote in *Golf in the Kingdom*, "Get to know the invader; it will help your game." To begin their self-inquiry, the players write down on worksheets their greatest fear on the golf course. The fear might be of looking like a duffer or of not reaching expectations. It might be a fear of failure or success, or of being secretly ridiculed by other players because of a poor performance. As one player once told me, "I'm afraid my warrior self (a term we were having a good time with that day) won't stand up to attack. I'm afraid of being labeled a wuss."

I clearly understand, however, that worrying about performance is a nearly universal concern. Beyond that, the critical first step, of course, is to directly address these fears—we all have our own separate fears—and get them out into the open. Unidentified and untamed fears are like toxic mold, they continue to grow as long as they are not held up to the light. Shine a little light on them, though, and they shrink and wither and lose their potency.

Often during our group workshops, we get into some great discussions about fear. Most of the players are relieved to hear that their colleagues often share the same fears. A common fear among many of the younger players who are hoping to make one of the professional tours is that they don't belong out there with the other competitors. They always seem to relax a little when they learn that most of the other players harbor similar concerns.

Making Fear Work for You

It isn't enough just to identify our fears, though. We also have to devise methods to counteract them. An upside to this is that tremendous energy is inherent in our fears. If we can harness that energy, we can often use it to help us develop the passion we need to attain high levels of performance.

Fear and trust are at the opposite ends of the inner-game continuum. Throughout this book, I talk about how to build trust and learn to cope with fear and negative emotions. We do that by developing a systematic approach that allows us to play automatically, with rapt attention to details related to performance and a minimum of time for fear to grow. One part of this systematic approach is the S.A.T. Process we discussed previously. By instantly evaluating our mis-hit shots, we shine a light directly on this potential germ of fear before it starts to grow. We identify the factors that caused us to mis-hit the shot, and then replace them with positive images and a synchronized feel and rhythm. Thus, one mis-hit shot does not lead directly to another. Fear is kept to a minimum, and positive emotions and trust replace it.

Our pre-shot routines are also critical to minimizing fear, because they keep our minds occupied with a simple, methodical process that leads to a trusting swing. There are other practices and processes in this book that all take dead aim at neutralizing fear. They include positive self-talk and imagining successful shots. Equally important is quality practice that simulates tournament situations, monitors the emotional mind and activates the imaginative mind in the process. This is a fundamental coaching technique used by nearly every great coach, including Bill Walsh. Bill, of course, won three Super Bowls with the San Francisco 49ers. Scores of his assistant coaches are now highly successful coaches in their own rights. It has been my privilege over the years to have held many discussions with him about athletic performance. His opinions were always well-thought-out, and his theories had been tested at the highest level of professional sports. I tended to listen when he talked.

"Every minute of every practice must connect directly to the game," Bill told me more than once. "Good players and coaches isolate every situation in a game and find a way to practice them. You see this type of contingency practice in every sport now." Bill shared much more on this subject that we'll present in later chapters.

Stronger than Fear

Also critical to banishing fear are trust in your equipment and, most importantly, the quality of the instruction you are receiving. You must trust your swing coach, your mental coach, and for some of you, conditioning coaches, agents, and advisors. You also must trust your ability to translate their teachings into processes that work for you.

Imagine, for a moment, the scales of justice. Fear of failure (of not living up to your expectations, of disapproval, of success, of missing a shot, etc.) is on one side of the scale, and these systemic processes, positive images, and self-talk are on the other. In total, you will become successful when your fear is outweighed by these other factors. It is important to understand that fear does not disappear; it is simply outweighed by the positive aspects of your practice, your outlook, and your inner trust.

Storytelling or *"The Sun was in My Eyes!"*

One of the most common and destructive habits of golfers (that can eat away at the foundation of your confidence) is what Fred

Shoemaker calls in *Extraordinary Golf,* "storytelling." Storytelling is a great enemy of self-confidence, because it is a complete denial of responsibility for each shot. Almost without exception, storytellers fail to reach their potential as golfers. Constant storytellers are also a pain in the neck to be around, because nothing is ever their fault.

All of us, at one time or another, tell stories. We rationalize and explain away our bad shots and bad rounds without taking ownership of them. A typical story I've heard over the years from pros and club players alike goes something like this: "Oh, man, I stayed up all night partying. We were drinking all night. Hell, I can't even see the ball this morning!" Such macho statements are usually followed up by some manly guffaws by playing partners, who are not doing the speaker any favors by validating his storytelling. The truth is, this is a simply a thinly-disguised excuse driven by fear. The story is meant to do two things. First, it gives the teller a way to avoid the fear that accompanies a competitive round by giving him an excuse for playing poorly, and second, it settles any question as to whether he is a partying dude!

Unfortunately, the story tells the more confident players two completely different things. First, that the teller hasn't much of an imagination, since this story has been used by storytellers for years, and second, that the teller is ripe for the picking. He's already making excuses. He's already giving in to fear by giving himself a green light to fail.

There are many, many types of stories, of course, and none of them do us any good. The players I work with know they are always to give me their scores first. No stories. Just the scores. Although I enjoy good storytelling in books and movies, on the golf course, being a good storyteller is not a good thing. Frankly, the better storyteller a player is, the less the chance that he will succeed in achieving his golfing goals.

Many players begin formulating their stories while they are still on the course. They spend as much time thinking up a good story to tell their friends as they do focusing on their game. Sometimes more! Telling stories may find you friends at the bar (although you should realize that they are accepting your story simply so you will accept theirs') and may be satisfying for a moment, but ultimately, telling stories drives away your self-confidence.

Storytelling is perhaps the hardest of the bad habits to break. Giving elaborate excuses as to why you didn't play up to your own expectations is like taking a drug. It feels good for a moment, but in the long run, it's terribly destructive. I know more than one player aspiring to the Tour who will not make it unless they give up their addictions to telling stories. Legendary UCLA basketball coach John Wooden states in *Pyramid of Success* that there shall be "no whining, complaining, or excuses." My students know, "No stories, please!"

If you find yourself telling stories (translated, that means making excuses for your round, or "I started triple, double, for a 77"), stop immediately and take responsibility for what you shot that day. Simply share your score, give a nonjudgmental rendition of your round, and then cap it off by saying you expect to play better tomorrow. Remember, your self-worth is not tied to your golf score. Better yet, give your score, and then add some positive things you did during your round. For example, you might say, "I shot an 80, but I made a long putt on 16, the tough par four, for a birdie." Just remember, while you are playing, golf should be the most important thing in the world to you, but when you are finished with your round, it should not be.

If you find yourself telling stories, check your attitude. Resist the temptation to tell everyone who will listen that you had seven three-putts. Most likely, you'll find you are being judgmental about your game, and fear has crept in—fear that you are not going to reach your golfing goals. Back off from the self-criticism and look for the joy in the game. Seek out what you did right today, even if you shot ten strokes over your handicap. Go back to the fundamental processes that you know work for you.

When you are finished with your round, and even while you are playing it, take full responsibility for every shot you hit. Mike Bowker, my co-author, was reminded of a story of when he was a young amateur playing in a tournament near Sacramento, California. He was playing with Phil Arrino, who was one of the best amateurs in the state at the time.

"I remember on the 18th hole I missed a four-foot putt to the left of the hole and then complained loudly that the ball hit a ball mark," Mike said with a laugh. "Phil looked me dead in the eye and said, 'You pulled that putt. Once you admit that, you'll improve.' I was mortified and angry at Phil for being so blunt, but over the years I realized he did me a tremendous favor. He showed me that top players won't put up with much storytelling, because they don't often do it themselves. He was giving me, in his way, one of the keys to success. I thought about his remark for a long time and became determined to take responsibility for my shots. Since that time I've tried hard not to tell stories, especially when I'm playing with Phil."

Fred Shoemaker suggests that storytelling is erosive to self-confidence, because it re-creates the emotional drama and trauma of the round. Some players repeat their stories ten or twenty times before they are finished. Confidence is likely to erode with each telling. Shoemakers says it is far more productive to debrief from a round, whether it is 66 or 86, by asking yourself nonjudgmental questions such as: "What did I learn today?"

Here is a list of 'stories' that you've probably heard. These are examples of negative ways in which players seek to shed pressure and fear. Feel free to add your favorite story, or the story of a frequent playing partner, to the list. They are ready-made excuses for the golfing failures that are sure to come:

- I haven't played in weeks! Don't expect much out of me today.
- My shoulder is so sore, I don't know if I can swing.
- I hit 15 greens, but had 38 putts.
- Did you see the shots I was hitting? My lesson yesterday was lousy.
- The course conditions were terrible.
- I can't play in a right-to-left wind.
- I got every bad break in the book out there.
- I'm making so much money at work that golf has taken a back seat.
- Putting on the greens was like putting on a waffle.
- I drove the ball into three divots today.
- Did you see who I was paired with?
- I need a new driver.
- I need a new putter.
- I need new irons.
- I need a new swing.

So what should you say after a round? I suggest you start with your score and then either accept the congratulations due or simply say with a shrug that you plan to play better tomorrow, and go off to prepare. One final thought to ponder: How often have you heard a player who shot a good round tell stories or make excuses?

Do I Belong Here?

I addressed this fear in earlier pages, but I want to come back to it, because it is a prevalent and powerful one among younger players chasing their dreams on the various junior, amateur, college, and professional tours. It can get pretty scary out there with grim-lipped players from all over the world competing against you. This fear can make players irrational at times, even mentally comparing their cars, clubs, and caddies to those of fellow players. "Who am I to think I can compete against these guys?" is a common thought. This kind of fear can cause all types of negative performance behavior.

A player I got to know during his excellent career on the University of the Pacific golf team was Sean Corte-Real. Sean was a unique player because of his experiences in his native country of Portugal. Sean remains the only golfer in Portuguese history to win the boy's and men's amateur titles (in 1996 and 2006 after regaining his amateur status) and then the men's professional title as well. He went on to play several years on the European Tour and now manages a five-star resort in southern Portugal, the Vila Sol. At the time this story takes place, however, he was a young tiger, trying to make his way through the ranks of European professionals. Because of his amateur pedigree, he had attracted the sponsorship of the BCB Bank in Portugal. This didn't exactly please his fellow Portuguese professionals, because Sean did most of his playing outside Portugal. Sponsorships were hard to come by in that country, and he was the object of some envy and resentment.

When he was 24 years old, his sponsors asked him to play in the Portuguese National Championship. Sean was nervous about it for two reasons. First, he would be playing in his home country, and his sponsors expected him to do well. Second, he thought he would be facing a group of resentful professionals who might give him a hard time.

"I told Glen that I thought these guys would try to eat me alive out there, and I was nervous about it," said Sean. "I had to prove I belonged, but it was going to be tough. I didn't think they'd even talk to me."

After a couple of discussions on the issue, Glen helped Sean develop the following strategy: "Glen told me that the first thing I should do when I got there was walk right up to these professionals and say, 'Hey, how are you doing? How's it going? Good to see you,' and things like that," said Sean. "That way I could be positive and get this thing out of the way. By chance, when I arrived at the course, most of the pros were seated around a long table having lunch. I looked at them with butterflies in my stomach, but I did what Glen suggested and stopped to talk to each player at the table. 'How are the kids? How is your club?' I meant it, too, and I think they could tell. They all responded well. From that moment on, it was as though a huge weight had been lifted off my shoulders. I knew I belonged. It was a great feeling. I had had that fear inside me for months. I worried about it all the time. Now, it was all gone. I broke the course record with a final round of 64 and won the tournament by one stroke. I have no doubt I was successful because I stood up to my fears."

How Do I Change My Deep Beliefs?

One of the challenges identified during the *Winning-the-Battle-Within* workshops is how to change negative emotions, beliefs, expectations, and identities that may have built up storytelling.

Many players remain at the same handicap level year after year, simply because they have come to believe that they are as good as they can ever become. Others have fallen into a pattern of not playing up to their expectations in tournaments. They may play well for a stretch of several holes, only to be followed by a blowout hole that sends them careening into negativity and yet another poor tournament round. It's almost as if they have programmed themselves to fail to live up to their own expectations.

Years ago, we called the failures that reside in our emotional memory "old tapes." Today, of course, we'd have to call them "old CDs." They are the memories that play again and again as we are victimized by pressures we put on ourselves. So the question becomes: How can we get rid of these old tapes? How do we change these negative deep beliefs and expectations and replace them with trust and joy?

First of all, let me reassure you that it can be done. As easily and systematically as we get rid of a nonproductive swing-feel after a mis-hit shot and replace it with a positive swing-feel (through the S.A.T. Process), we can eliminate negative deep beliefs and replace them with positive ones.

Positive deep beliefs about our games are formed when several factors come together. Many of these have already been noted, but I would put them in a different order here, because the first thing you must do is become aware of and dislodge the old negative beliefs that are holding you back. The changes you can make that will allow a substantive transformation to take place most often begin with a complete belief in your instructors. This holds true for both your mental and swing coach. You must believe that you are doing the right thing, that the instruction you are receiving is fundamentally sound, and that it will make you a better player. A powerful belief in your coaches is an effective key to replacing old negative beliefs with positive ones. You must be open to the teaching and be armed with a plan of action to move yourself toward your golfing goals. In his book, *Mastery,* George Leonard, an expert on sports performance and the human-potential movement, calls it "surrendering to the teaching/learning moment." It is the ability to suppress your ego, and instead, strive to master the skills so you can advance to the next competitive level. Leonard adds that although performance seems to be stuck on a plateau, when in pursuit of 'mastery,' one must have the confidence to stay with practice regimens that consistently enhance learning and promote improvement. With patience and commitment, a leap to the next performance plateau is inevitable.

The pathway to peak performance is not an easy one, although some improvements will come quickly. The hills you must climb can be steep and razor thin and you may fall off from time to time. Don't worry about it when it happens; it's simply part of the success process. If you trust your instructors and the internal processes you've established, you will know how to jump back on the path and your performances will continue to improve.

The S.A.T. Process is a critical component to reaching peak performance and to having as much fun as possible while performing. Having fun doesn't mean a commitment to telling jokes, goofing around, or losing focus. It simply means allowing yourself to find joy in a well-hit shot and in the anticipation of hitting your next shot with perfect feel and rhythm. Men, especially, have to begin to give themselves full permission to enjoy the sights, smells, textures, and events of each day.

Developing Your Golfing Identity

In my workshops, I usually have the players answer some questions that help them establish a positive golfing mindset to take with them to the course. Answering these questions is another way to help confidence grow. You might want to answer them yourself on a piece of paper, so you can refer back to them just before you play an important match. It is a great way to prepare yourself for the battle and to refresh your positive deep beliefs. Remember, there are no right answers, just honest reflections on the way you think, imagine, and concentrate while playing. (Also, see the Self-Improvement

Questionnaire in the appendix.) Here are the questions:
- How did you feel just before starting to play your all-time best golf round?
- What did you say to yourself just before your last good round?
- What did you say to yourself during the round?
- What did you say after a mis-hit shot to help you recover mentally?
- How did you handle feelings of fear or anxiety that occurred during the round?
- How did you handle the pressure of playing several good holes in a row?
- What was your primary mental imagery during the day?
- Were you thinking of a particular phrase or song, or were you just enjoying the scenery?

Rather than trying to re-create these things exactly from one round to the next, use these positive thoughts and images to build the foundation for a positive feel and approach to your next round. Although every round will be different, you should allow each round to define itself, while always relying on a foundation of systematic processes that you trust.

The Mindset for Excellence

Here are a few thoughts that may help you build positive deep beliefs that are a distinctive feature of confidence. I developed them with Kevin Sverduk, an applied sport psychologist at Long Beach State near Los Angeles. Kevin has a Ph.D. in the subject, and we have spent years working together investigating the components of quality practice and the journey toward excellence in sport performance.

- Learn to let go of attachments to results. This leads to a cycle of harsh self-judgment and self-doubt. You cannot control results. What you can control is your mastery over the internal processes you are developing. Does this mean that you shouldn't try to 'will the ball into the hole?' Of course not. Ben Hogan's stare sometimes scared the ball so badly it dared not miss the hole, or so it seemed. In truth, 'willing the ball into the hole' is simply a positive mental process that allows players to stroke the putt with full trust and confidence.

- Letting go provides an opportunity to experience golf to its fullest. Letting go is the only true pathway to gaining control.

- The pursuit of excellence requires a relentless commitment, is fraught with adversity, and is a lifelong journey. Many start down the path, but few have the courage and discipline to stay on it.

- Finding the right path is as important as learning to stay on it. Select mentors who understand elite performance, who can help you find the path, and who can provide you with skills to continue your ascent.

Mental Toughness

Mental toughness comes in many forms and is another prominent trait of confidence. To me, the father or mother who works hard all day during the week, comes home to be with the children, and fully engages in loving and nurturing them is mentally tough. Resisting the temptation to move to Hawaii and live alone in a grass hut, when your teenager gets his nose pierced and wrecks the family car all in one day, requires true mental toughness.

Golf-wise, though, mental toughness is much like a jazz riff that stays in an unhurried rhythm all night long. Mental toughness means playing the game with evenness and grace. It means that every internal process you have built into your golf identity is operating at full capacity and in clear harmony with your deep beliefs.

In one of his many inner-game articles, Tom Kubistant, a Reno-based sport psychologist, provides an excellent way to understand what he likes to call the mental toughness-softness continuum. From Kubistant's concept, I like to draw two circles with a horizontal line between them. One circle I label 'toughness,' and the other, 'softness.' Inside the toughness circle, I write the words: concentration, resiliency, creativity, deep inner beliefs, nonjudgmental evaluations, trusting swings, and patience. Inside the softness circle, I write the two major categories that lead to on-course tactical errors: carelessness and trying too hard. Then I write the ways in which they are manifested on the golf course, including: tension, fear, expectation, harsh self-judgment, anger, impatience, and focusing on results.

This is a good exercise to underscore those elements that must come together for us to gather and maintain the mental toughness we need to reach and maintain peak performance. Just as you can choose to become confident, you can choose to become mentally tough. By the way, don't confuse rudeness or abrasiveness with being mentally tough. Few golfers in the history of golf have been tougher mentally than Lee Trevino, yet he was also one of the most congenial players ever to grace the PGA TOUR.

Mental Toughness in Thirty Seconds or Less

If you want to become mentally tougher on the golf course, raise your right hand and repeat after me, keeping your affirmations in the first person, present tense.

1. I am not judgmental toward my own shots or scores. In fact, without hesitation, I review, replace, and refocus.

2. I do not tell stories before, during, or after a round. I debrief and learn.

3. I do not let my expectations get in my way. My expectations are realistic and serve to motivate and focus me.

4. I do not give in to frustration. Instead, I focus on my internal processes, change the negative emotion, and replace ineffective swings with effective ones.

5. After every round, I ask myself, "What did I do right and what did I learn today?"

6. I do not like playing poorly, but I do not fear it.

7. I identify and recognize pressure and fear when it arises, then I refocus on my internal processes and swing tension free.

8. I enjoy playing well; I do not fear it.

9

GREAT ADVICE FROM GREAT COACHES

Some years ago, when I was still in college, we suffered though an unusually wet spring in California. It rained day and night for weeks. I was sharing a house with another student, who kept coming home late every afternoon soaking wet. I would look up from my studies, and he would come through the front door, shoes squishing with water and clothes stuck to his body as if he had just climbed out of a swimming pool. Finally, I asked him what in the world he was doing every afternoon that caused him to get drenched like that. He looked at me kind of funny and said, "Practicing."

"In this downpour?" I asked him. He shrugged. "I love to practice," was all he said. He went on to become a legend on the PGA TOUR, and I always thought it had something to do with his extraordinary commitment to practice and to his game. His name was Ken Venturi.

As most of you know, Ken won the United States Open in dramatic fashion and to become one of the best players in golf until a progressive disease in his hands forced him to quit at age thirty-three. What many of you may not know is that Ken had a speech impediment as a child and was reluctant to talk much as a young man. Determined to overcome his challenge, Ken spent countless hours practicing how to speak clearly. His relentless dedication and practice paid off as he spent the next four decades as one of the outstanding golf broadcasters in the history of the sport. Quality practice is the foundation of almost all meaningful achievement. Ken Venturi is a perfect example of this, in these two aspects of his life.

Performance Tips From Bill Walsh and Pete Carroll

Nobody believes in quality practice more than Bill Walsh and Pete Carroll. Corporations paid Bill tens of thousands of dollars to consult with them about what it takes to win in a competitive market. I greatly appreciate the fact that both of these great coaches, with whom I've worked for many years, were kind enough to agree to share their inside thoughts about practice and performance in this chapter.

Bill was an avid amateur golfer, and he saw a tremendous overlap between football and golf when it came to the value of quality practice. The following are some of his and Pete's observations and suggestions involving practice as well as some tips on how an athlete should prepare to join the Winner's Circle.

Bill Walsh

Is practice important?

"Well, let me tell you a little story. When Joe Montana was in his late thirties, he still asked me to watch and evaluate his practices. He would be out there working hard on his footwork and on different passing patterns. He would ask me to assess the various aspects of his practice, and he would always practice simulated game situations. He knew exactly why he was out there. Even though it was clear at that point that he was a future Hall-of-Fame quarterback who had already won four Super Bowls, he felt he could still improve. It proves you should never feel you have mastered all your skills. This is especially true in golf where there are so many different skills required of you."

How connected is practice to game performance?

"They are inseparable. A television announcer at Wimbledon once asked Pete Sampras, who was then in his prime, if he elevated his game during one especially tough match. 'No,' Pete said. 'I just try to serve like I do in practice. How can you elevate your game in the middle of a competition? You can only do what you did in practice.'

"To me, that says everything. Practice is where you set the stage for game performance. Through practice, you prepare and build the confidence you need. Quality practice is essential to quality game performance."

What constitutes quality practice?

"We called it 'contingency practice,' and you see it in all sports now. What we tried to do was anticipate every possible situation that could arise in a real game, and we would practice it. For example, we would pretend we had the ball on the opponent's ten-yard line with just a few seconds left and we were six behind. We'd choose a play, and the team would practice it until we had it down. We'd practice two-minute drills on defense and offense. We prepared for every situation we could think of, so we would give ourselves every chance we could to win. Golfers must do the same. You have to practice hitting out of bad lies and good lies and sand traps and rough and hitting fades and draws. You have to imagine yourself in tournament situations—maybe you are two behind with four to play or one up with one to play. What shots will you hit? What if you are on the 18th hole tied for the lead and you land in a bad lie? Will you be prepared mentally to hit that shot? If your contingency practice is complete, you will be.

"I remember one game, while I was coach of the 49ers, when we had the ball on the opponent's seven-yard line with seven seconds left. We didn't even have to call a timeout. The team knew what play to run and how to run it because we had practiced for that contingency so many times. Of course, it didn't hurt that we had Joe Montana passing to Jerry Rice on the play, but any confusion can wreck a play no matter who is performing it. Any time during practice that you aren't preparing for a game-time situation is usually wasted. This doesn't mean you will always succeed, but you are giving yourself the best possible chance."

Why are expectations dangerous?

"It's easy to stay in the present before you've experienced success (in golf, success might mean breaking one hundred for the first time). Once you've been successful, however, you begin to battle expectations. Expectations will take you out of the present, if you let them. You can't think about outcomes; you have to concentrate on your next shot. The old cliché, 'take one game at a time,' is repeated so often for a reason. It is simply a way to remind yourself to stay in the present."

How important are goals?

"Goals are critical, but they must be reasonable and achievable. When I first joined the 49ers, they were a derelict team and organization. They weren't good at all. But, we focused on improving, one game at a time, and we reached goal after goal until we achieved our ultimate goal—winning a Super Bowl. Had we set a goal of winning the Super Bowl our first year, we would have been crushed. We had to establish a standard of performance through quality, contingency practice and then advance our goals every year."

How do you develop a successful game strategy?

"All plans and strategies should be developed well in advance of the game or tournament. These should be created and designed with enough time left before game day that the elements of that strategy can be practiced. A golfer should have a strategy ready before reaching the first tee. You create a game plan, and then you don't look back. As Pete Sampras said, you can't change your game in the middle of a competition."

But doesn't this quash improvisation and an athlete's instinct?

"No, just the opposite. All elite athletes have superior intuition and instincts. The key, if you are a coach, is to put your athletes in positions to best utilize their instincts. A golfer, of course, must prepare to put himself into positions to use his imagination and superior improvisational skills. You do this through proper preparation. If you are certain about your fundamentals because you repeated them often in practice, and if you are confident in your strategy because you developed it carefully in a calm atmosphere before the competition, then you are in a perfect position to fully utilize your intuitive skills because you aren't preoccupied with those things. If you haven't practiced properly, or if you haven't developed a complete game strategy, intuition and instinct can be buried under an avalanche of thoughts about mechanics and doubts about strategy."

Pete Carroll

Pete, who was one of my best students at the University of Pacific, is one of the foremost thinkers among today's coaches. Pete was a very good football player—he played safety for the UOP Tigers—but he stood out for me because he was one of the most inquisitive students I've ever had. After graduating, Pete began a coaching odyssey that connected him with important mentors, including

Walsh. He eventually became the head coach for the New England Patriots for three years and is now the celebrated head coach for the incredibly successful University of Southern California football team. USC won consecutive national titles before losing its bid for a three-peat in the memorable game against the University of Texas in 2006. They continued their incredible run with dominating victories in the 2007 and 2008 Rose Bowls.

Pete and I have stayed in close contact over the years, and I've been privileged to be a part of his quest for deeper knowledge of the subject of athletes and peak performance. He never stops thinking and working and putting his ideas into practice, and as a result, he has become one of the most successful and sought-after coaches in America. Like Walsh, Carroll is completely sold on the concept of contingency practice. Here are some points of wisdom that Pete shared with us.

How critical is imagination in conducting a quality practice?

"It's everything. Whether you are practicing football, golf, or any other sport, you have to bring lots of imagination to the practice field. You have to imagine everything while you practice. You have to put yourself into every simulated game situation you can think of and practice the same things you will be doing when the game or tournament is on the line. You have to feel like you've been there before. You should practice every situation you might find yourself in when the pressure is really on. That way you'll be more comfortable during the actual competition. For example, you might imagine you have a one-shot lead going into the last hole. What club will you hit off the tee? How will your approach shot feel? Maybe you have to get your chip shot up and down to win. Maybe you have to make a putt to tie, or hit a drive with water along the left side. There should be no contingency that you haven't practiced and prepared for by the time you leave the practice tee or putting green."

How important is visualization to achieving your goals?
"Man, you're asking me easy questions. That's the first step toward peak performance. You have to know what you want to become and then see yourself becoming it. What you see yourself achieving is usually what you will achieve. You figure out what you want to become, work your tail off, and you can do anything."

How critical should you be of your players?
"Most athletes don't respond well to negative feedback. Do we evaluate? Of course. We'll look at it and determine how to correct it and figure out how to take the next positive step. We don't spend any time at all on the negative aspects—for example, showing a player what he did wrong. We only talk about how to do it right the next time.

"One part of football that is similar to golf is the kicking game. We never focus on what a kicker did wrong when he misses a field goal. We may evaluate the kick and notice that he was too close to the ball with his plant foot, but the emphasis is on the fact that next time he should plant his foot two inches from the ball, not one inch. Golfers are the same way. It is a total waste of time to focus on the things you did wrong. The worst thing you can do as a coach is call one of your players a 'dumb-ass.' There just isn't anything constructive about that at all. Golfers tend to call themselves similar or worse names from time to time, but they should realize there isn't anything constructive about doing that. It's critical to focus on the positive construct of your next play or your next shot. Just figure out what you need to do to hit it right, and then go do it." I often recommend that golf professionals follow this same procedure and teach and demonstrate only what they want their students to do

Should practice be fun?

"Well, it's not always fun in football, because there is conditioning, especially early in the season. But, at least a good portion of the practice should be fun, because the players know that what they are doing is critical to achieving their goals. Everyone should always know exactly why they are practicing this drill or repeating that play. In golf, you should know exactly what you are going to achieve by hitting the next ball on the practice range. You are preparing for a specific game situation. That makes practice a lot more exciting, because in your imagination, you can simulate the feelings of actually playing in a tournament. If you are clear on your goals and you practice properly, you will enjoy the journey a great deal more."

What should you do when things go wrong?

"First of all, you never panic. You should believe in your practice and in your strategy. You stick with the things that you know work. If you stick with it, you'll find a reservoir of confidence and get back on track. Rick Barry, the NBA-Hall-of-Fame forward for the San Francisco Warriors, once told a reporter that he knew he was a 48-percent shooter from the floor. That's why he never panicked when things went wrong. 'I was confident that I would reach my shooting percentage sooner or later,' said Barry. 'I figured if I missed my first ten shots, look out.'"

Winning Time

One of my favorite expressions and concepts comes from Bob Thomason, the highly successful mens' basketball coach at UOP. Bob is also a strict proponent of contingency practice. He spends nearly all his practice time simulating game situations, especially during what he calls 'winning time.' For Bob and his basketball team, winning time is the final four minutes of the game. Bob is also a very good amateur golfer, a dangerous two handicapper who can really play. He thinks of winning time on the golf course as being the last three or four holes.

"We work hard on every contingency that could arise during winning time," Bob says. "Golfers should do the same. An example that comes to mind is Jean Van de Velde, the player who lost the 1999 British Open by triple-bogeying the 18th hole on the final day. He obviously didn't prepare well for winning time, because he took a three-shot lead into that narrow final hole and still hit a driver off the tee. That put him deep in the right rough where he tried to reach the green rather than laying up short. Had he imagined all the contingencies during practice, he would have known what to do coming to the 18th with a lead. He would have prepared mentally to hit a safe iron shot into the fairway. I think he came to the tee and on the spur of the moment decided to hit the driver because that was the club that had been working for him all week. Clearly, he didn't trust it, though. Standing on the tee with all that pressure on him wasn't the time to be making up strategy. You have to imagine all the possibilities of winning time in the quiet, relaxed atmosphere of the practice tee and have your strategy airtight before you step onto the course."

Thomason also reflected that the ultimate golf practice would be for two or more players to compete in a friendly way. "That would make it fun," he said. "You could have contests to see who could get closest to various targets. This kind of competition would get a player as close as possible to simulating the pressure of a tournament."

I agree with Bob, especially for those players who have outgoing natures and enjoy the camaraderie of the other competitors.

Some golfers, though, are of solitary natures, and a team approach to practice could actually be detrimental to them. In the end, it is important to know yourself well enough to construct the type of practice that is most productive for you. However, it is clear that contingency practice—the simulation of tournament conditions and imagining the course you are about to play and the exact shots you'll be required to hit—is crucial to achieving peak performance. You should know your exact strategy for every situation in which you might find yourself during winning time as you come down the stretch in the tournament.

When it comes to proper practice, your own imagination, as Pete pointed out, is perhaps the most important club in your bag. It not only prepares you for both the shots and the emotions you may face during the tournament, it also makes practice more fun.

10

THE THREE STAGES
OF MOTOR LEARNING:

Scientific Insights That Will Help Your Game

It wouldn't be any fun for me to write this book, if I didn't plunge into the science of motor learning at least a little bit. I promise you this is a short chapter, and I won't quiz you when it's done, but you might find some of the information in the following pages helpful when it comes to understanding and analyzing your practice efforts and lessons.

Much of the material I discuss here comes from motor-learning research and sport-psychology texts. It involves some academic, sport-psychology talk, but I figure you will forgive me for it. All of the concepts presented have been battle-tested in sport settings and are endorsed by a cadre of great coaches, golf teachers, and golfers who have helped with this book.

If you are terribly anxious to get to the actual practice drills, however, and if you are reading this on the last sunny day of the season, you have my permission to skip this chapter (just for now!) and go on to the next chapter which outlines a number of actual practice routines, many of which you may have never encountered before. But, before you do that, you must promise to return to this chapter later, because it provides some valuable insight into how to get the most out of your lessons and practice sessions.

How the Mind Learns Sport Skills

I touched on the learning process earlier in the book, but it is worth bringing up the three stages again, because they are keys to understanding how golfers should practice, learn, and perform. The three stages are: cognitive, associative, and autonomous learning. These are adapted from Richard Schmidt's *Motor Learning and Performance.* If you coach or teach golf, I encourage you to get a copy of Schmidt's book and learn as much as you can about the stages of learning. Understanding the stages is crucial to the learning and teaching process.

Stage One: Cognitive Learning

All learning begins with the cognitive stage, especially the learning of a sport skill. You know this stage quite well. We all do. This type of learning occurs when the coach or instructor explains and describes the skill, sometimes with the aid of a computer screen, a set of instructions, or a live demonstration. Whether you are new to golf or making a mid-life swing change, the thinking, cognitive, part of your brain must first try to get an idea of the new movement patterns.

Cognitive learning is characterized by conscious attention to the details of movement. It is a necessary step in the learning process, but because you spend so much time thinking about the new movement, it can appear stiff, tense, and halting. But, conscious attention to this level of detail can also be a monstrous trap.

The bones of many a luckless golfer lay bleaching in the waste-land of the cognitive process. They are the unlucky ones who have failed to move beyond this step. (Good golfers like to compete against these guys, because they often wilt under pressure.) Those who become mired in the cognitive process get hooked on tech-nique and on the myth that somewhere in the cognitive process lies *the answer* to the riddle of the mechanically perfect swing. They long to believe that the key to the golfing kingdom can be found in the cognitive arena. There is no end to the golfing gurus in magazines and on television who fan that particular fire. Yet this stage—the conscious, analytical, mechanical phase—is just the beginning. It is certainly nowhere near the finish line. Staying in this stage will rob you of sustained improvement and reaching your peak performance.

External Feedback

During the cognitive phase, all the information you get about your swing comes through external or extrinsic feedback. That is, it comes through the attention, praise, analysis, or criticism from your pro or whoever is looking at your swing at the time. If you are practicing by yourself, it may come from the flight of the ball or perhaps a stationary video camera.

There is no question that extrinsic feedback is important. It is critical when you are learning new skills or when you are working on alignment issues. Before you've developed the internal feel of a particular shot, it's useful to receive external feedback about the quality of your execution. But, external feedback can become a narcotic, if it is used too much. It can become psychologically addicting to rely entirely on coaches, friends, or magazine articles for their comments and input. Relying solely on external feedback is seductive because it erases the accountability for our own games.

I'm sure you've heard players, who are having a bad round, blaming a recent lesson and perhaps even the local pro. The danger of this is that once personal accountability evaporates, significant improvement becomes impossible. The external feedback that occurs during the cognitive stage of motor learning should take place at the beginning of the improvement cycle, not the end. Occasionally, a player, in cooperation with a trusted teacher, will return to the cognitive stage for a quick tune-up. One should stay in the cognitive stage only briefly and make every attempt to get back to automatic play as soon as possible.

Observation, Imitation, and Experimentation

Many sport skills are learned best through a progression of observation, imitation, and experimentation, after external feedback has started the process. Many elite golfers subscribe to a learning process of observing the swing movement, imitating what was observed, and then experimenting with the movement until satisfied with the results. This last step is crucial because that is when you take ownership of the skill. It is no longer the instructor's skill; it is yours, because you have modified it to meet your needs. Once you take ownership, you become accountable for executing that particular shot. The outcome of the shot is yours and yours alone. As I've mentioned before, accountability is a critical step toward constant improvement, automatic play, and ultimate peak performance.

During the observation stage, you may watch a live demonstration, a videotape, a sequence of pictures on television or a computer screen, or simply assimilate a verbal explanation.

Every lesson should contain quality time for you to imitate the movement you've just seen or heard. This should include encouragement for you to rehearse the swing, while you imagine the shot and gain a feel for the swing. It's important during experimentation for the teacher to withhold feedback, so the player can attend to internal feedback as a consequence of the movement.

Finally, you should experiment with this new knowledge by repeating the movement. You should use continued imagery and focus on the feel of the swing. Small tweaks may be necessary before you feel comfortable with the new movement and begin to achieve positive results.

Internal Feedback

Athletes receive this information as a natural consequence of moving. It is captured and then provided by the athlete's own sensory system. Meredith, in *Life Before Death: A Spiritual Experience,* devotes a chapter to 'sensuous sportsmen.' He defines an advanced interval-feedback system, explaining that imagination is our capacity to organize mental representations of the movement before performing the movement. David Cook, a sport psychologist based in San Antonio, Texas, says, "See the shot, feel the swing that matches what you see, and then trust what you see and feel. Such language-action phrases help develop your internal-feedback system so you can play in your imagination and sense rhythmic swings in advance." Cook has worked with a number of players, including Steve Lowry, Tom Pernice, and Casey Martin.

Internal or intrinsic feedback can occur in variety of forms. It can come as a matter of feel or as a clear, internal image of the swing. Most players can correctly predict how they hit the ball— left, right, or down the middle—even when they don't see the ball leave the club head. If they are in touch with their sensory system, they can also tell you how the club reacted during the swing. The more coherent the sensory response, the more synchronized the swing will become. Each player generates a wealth of information through this intrinsic, sensory-information bank. Most often, however, players do not take advantage of this information. It is usually ignored in favor of any external feedback that may come from the flight of the ball, a coach, or even playing partners. Peak performance, though, is built largely on intrinsic feedback during the round itself. As with all the other aspects of the game, it is critical that golfers practice accessing their intrinsic information bank so that it will become an automatic process during competitive rounds. External feedback can be a motivating tactic of a good coach, and it can lead to important improvements. But, it is internal feedback that provides the self-sustaining lifeblood to all athletes during performance. The wisdom to hit good golf shots resides within each golfer and not in the heads of their instructors.

Richard Keefe, who has written extensively on the central nervous system's process for learning and performing golf skills, writes in his book, *Toward the Sweet Spot,* "The better your sense of feel for the rhythm and motion of the club head, the better your form will be."

Internal Feedback and the S.A.T. Process

One of the reasons successful players can exercise the S.A.T. Process in a matter of seconds is that they are fully accessing their internal information bank. They know almost instantaneously whether their strategy was solid, and they often can sense whether or not their aim was proper. Finally, they often know before they have completed their swings whether there was tension or trust in them. These players have opened the door to this internal information rather than barricading it with conscious, external thoughts on technique.

Keefe has spent a great deal of time studying the speed with which superior athletes are able to integrate external information (yardage, wind, etc.) and internal information (seeing, feeling, etc.)

without cognitive or emotional interference. He found that visual and kinesthetic sensory feedback often arrive simultaneously with a strategy decision.

I've heard top golfers say, "I've got this one." You've probably had that feeling yourself, many times. It is almost inevitably followed by a good, if not great, golf shot. Most players haven't given much thought to the process that produces this wonderful feeling—they think it just happens. The golfers in my workshops get pretty excited when they realize that they have it within their power to make it happen. It takes work, though. In order to allow the speedy integration of psycho-physiological data to take place in competition, your must practice the integration of internal feedback.

Any player can access this internal information, but it requires effort and practice. A good practice session for golfers should be as much about internal process as about technique. Successful players will tell you they practice more on feel and rhythm and hitting specific types of shots, and even on their pre-shot routines, than on specific swing techniques.

Contingency Practice

The entire concept of intrinsic feedback ties in directly with the passion that Coach Walsh and Coach Carroll have for contingency practices. For more than a decade, I have maintained that golf teachers and coaches can learn a great deal about quality practice from team sport coaches. Contingency or simulated practice has been the theme of many workshops based on *Winning the Battle Within*.

Players who are consciously thinking about mechanics while battling opponents over the final few holes do not win golf tournaments. Tournaments are won by those who trust their swings and are confident about executing learned processes through their pre-shot and post-shot routines. They are won by those who have full access to their internal-information banks and utilize the information. They are won by those who play in their imaginative minds, which is the corridor to what is often referred to as 'being in the zone.'

For golfers, contingency practice of simulated game situations requires access to that same intrinsic environment. If players rarely, if ever, reach peak performance by consciously thinking about technique during their swings, why should any golfer concentrate solely on external technique on the practice tee? Yet, we all know that most golfers do exactly that. They stand in one area, hitting ball after ball, providing themselves with little internal feedback, perhaps only an occasional reference to tempo and rhythm. Often, they take nothing more than a cursory inventory of external-feedback information, and that is usually the flight of the ball. How many times on the golf course do you stand and hit 30 balls in a row with the same club at the same target? The answer should shed some light on just how valuable that type of practice is in terms of helping you prepare for real-time playing conditions. (There is some value in hitting 30 seven irons in a row when you are learning a new motor skill. But, too many players forget that they also have to learn how to make that shot on the course, where they will have only one chance to hit it.)

McCarron's 40-Minute, 20-ball Approach

When I first started working with Scott, he practiced like most of the other amateur players he had competed with over the years. He would grab a bucket of balls and blast away, sometimes not even bothering to take careful aim. His enormous talent was not being developed in this manner. After we worked together for a few months, he changed his practice routine dramatically and for the better.

Before I go any further with this story, I should point out that Scott always customized whatever information I gave him so that it fit his game. He has always made the information his own, taking full accountability and responsibility for every shot he hits. It has been fun to work with him, because he clearly understands the value of contingency practice.

Scott's chipping practice is a perfect example of the disciplined, contingency-based routine that defines his entire approach to practice. He often takes one ball, drops it off the green, and then goes through his pre-shot routine before pitching to the hole. Next, he takes off his glove and marks his ball, if it isn't within two feet of the hole. After that, he lines up his putt and goes through another pre-shot routine before putting the ball into the hole. In his imagination, he places himself on a particular course in a particular tournament to simulate, as closely as possible, the feelings and emotions he will have during the real competition. After holing the putt, he puts his glove back on, drops another ball, and begins the chipping process all over again. Often, it will take him more than 40 minutes to chip 20 balls. But, every practice shot he hits is important, and he is fully engaged with it, just as he is with every shot he hits in a tournament.

Many players, when I tell them about Scott's disciplined regimen, say it sounds to them like a surefire way to take the fun out of the game. But, in truth, Scott's imagination is so actively engaged during this time that he gains a sense of deep satisfaction and enjoyment out of the process. In a way, it is much like reading a great novel that takes you away from the everyday world into an imaginary world where anything becomes possible. The inner strength developed during this process is exactly what you need to join the winner's circle. Scott has used his to bank more than twelve million dollars in career earnings.

The Final Two Stages of Learning

Following the cognitive stage of learning come the final two stages—the Associative and the Autonomous. These two stages often separate professionals from amateurs. Professionals, although perhaps not always consciously aware of it, have assimilated the external feedback of the cognitive stage and have developed a feel for the swing and the game to a point where it all has become automatic. Most likely, you know exactly what I mean, because on occasions you've reached this automatic stage yourself. Think back to your best games ever, and I'll bet you remember standing over the ball with total confidence that all you had to do was pull the trigger and your swing was going to work. What I'm saying here is you can choose to get to that stage more often. Here is a quick look at the final two stages.

Stage Two: Associative Learning

During this phase, the learner practices the skill to the point that it is performed both accurately and consistently. The skill becomes a motor program. Proprioceptive control and kinesthetic feel gradually replace conscious control of movement, which was dominant during the cognitive learning phase. The golfer is developing an internal-feedback system, and is likely to report to the teacher, "I'm beginning to feel it!"

Stage Three: Autonomous Learning

As the term implies, performance during this phase is quite automatic, and the learner requires very little conscious thought or attention to the details of movement. The internal-feedback system for the skill is developed. In fact, asking highly skilled performers to consciously focus on the content of their movements will seriously disrupt the synchronization of the movement and impair performance.

Your goal as an evolving golfer should be to get to the autonomous stage as quickly and efficiently as possible. The following chapter provides a series of practice routines that are tailored to helping you learn to trust your swing and play more fully in your imaginative mind. They are designed to help you play automatically. You'll undoubtedly like some of the routines more than others—everybody has favorites—and I encourage you to modify them in any way that best suits your game. Have fun with them, and work your imaginative mind as you would your biceps or your deltoids in the gym. If you are like the overwhelming majority of the players I work with, you will feel your inner game strengthening almost immediately.

Michael Murphy once wrote a phrase that I thought captured this concept perfectly: "The inner body is not bound to the physical frame it inhabits. It is far more elastic and free, more like a flame than a rock." As you hone your skills, allow the flame to grow. With that, I say enjoy the practice drills that start on the next page—and then go burn up the course.

11

QUALITY PRACTICE:

Powering Your Inner Game

Recently, I held a *Winning-the-Battle-Within* seminar at Elkhorn Country Club in Stockton, California, and invited a number of Northern California's top golf professionals and golf coaches to attend. For the afternoon session, we all went to the practice area where McCarron, and several other professional golfers with whom I work, showed everyone how to execute some of the drills I'll describe in this chapter. During one drill, we set up a surprise for the audience. I had asked Eric Jones, the World Seniors' Long-Drive Champion, to sit in the bleachers with everyone else. (In addition to his long-driving skills, Eric is a golf professional teaching in the Bay Area and has completed a master's degree in applied sport psychology.) Most of the audience was not aware of Eric's accomplishments and McCarron was to act as if he were picking someone at random from the crowd to execute a drill with a driver. Of course, he picked Eric, who played his part well, grumbling as if he felt unlucky to be singled out to hit shots in front of his fellow professionals.

Scott teed up about six balls, explained the drill, and asked Eric to hit the balls in rapid succession. Our idea, of course, was for Eric to 'wow' the crowd with his prodigious length with the driver. But, what happened next was even more intriguing and instructive than we had anticipated. Eric's first shot was a hard hook into the netting. His next two were hit a mile long, but they were hit so far to the right that the audience wasn't aware of how far he was hitting the ball. Eric managed one down the middle, but then he pushed the next two over the driving range fence. By the end of the drill, he was clearly frustrated. He felt he had let Scott and me down by not impressing the crowd with his giant, long drives.

Scott, though, knew exactly what had happened. After I introduced Eric as the Seniors' Long-Drive Champion and let the audience know we were having some fun with them, Eric admitted that he had been trying too hard. He said he was pressing to uphold his end of the surprise.

"But, in a way, the drill worked perfectly," Scott pointed out. "It showed that Eric was judging each shot as he hit it, and this judgment process got in the way of his next shot. He wasn't tension-free, because he was pressing so hard. So, the drill worked. It is designed to show the difference between consciously judging your shots and just letting go."

After saying this, Scott teed up a few more balls. "This time," he told Eric, "don't think about the shot you previously hit. Don't let the judgment of your last shot linger, just set up, get into your rhythm, and concentrate on the shot before you."

Eric was visibly relaxed by Scott's words. He began swinging with rhythm and a tension-free tempo, and before long he was blasting balls 350 yards and more beyond the fence at the back of the practice range. His entire body looked relaxed and this time he did 'wow' the crowd. Taking the judgment and conscious thought out of his routine was the key to reaching his peak performance.

Innovative Approach to Practice

In this chapter, I introduce you to a new way to practice that takes conscious thinking out of the equation. These drills are ones you've likely never tried before, even if you are an experienced golfer. They are designed to help you learn to trust your swing, play more fully in your imaginative mind, and swing automatically. The inner-game drills include methods to improve tempo, rhythm, and the synchronization of your swing. Others introduce you to 'variable' and 'random' practice. You'll find specific tips on practicing your short game and putting. Each drill is explained so you can implement it yourself or do it with another person. The best part is that they are elements of contingency practice and are geared toward helping you simulate a competitive round.

One of the biggest differences I've seen between amateur and professional golfers is in their approaches to practice routines. Most amateurs have a simple approach to practice—they hit a bucket or two without any specific goal for the practice session except a vague search for some mechanical-swing key that they hope will transform their game. I often hear players exclaim with excitement that they have 'found it!' The 'it' is always some mechanical element, such as standing closer to (or farther from) the ball, a different grip, or maybe a shift in swing plane.

As most of us know from frustrating experience, the euphoria we feel when we 'find it' on the practice tee almost always disappears on the course. It might survive a round or two before disappearing, but most often 'it' is gone long before the day is over.

Practice that involves repeating a specific swing pattern without interruption is called 'blocked practice.' Most of the feedback during these sessions is external, with much of it involving the flight of the ball. We might hit ten five-irons in a row, then ten seven irons, then ten wedge shots, etc. Although some internal feedback occurs in terms of tempo, rhythm, and release at impact, what most of us are really seeking is a mechanical key that will allow us to hit multiple, solid shots.

Blocked practice has limited use, however, and at least one major pitfall. Hitting balls in repetitive fashion can cause golfers to be overconfident about how well they've learned certain motor skills. Standing in one area hitting the same kinds of shots from good lies is a great way to take all the tension out of your swing. There is little concern over the outcome of any one shot during this type of practice, so the mental environment does not mimic the one you face when actually playing the course. Rarely will you find yourself in a situation during a competition on the golf course when one shot doesn't matter. The relaxed state in which you find yourself during blocked practice is artificial, and therefore the practice itself is of limited use. Can you imagine Joe Montana standing behind the center and throwing passes without taking one-step, three-step, or five-step drops?

As I've mentioned, blocked practice does have a role, however, when you are learning a new skill. It is often used with your golf instructor, in the first stage of learning, when the emphasis is on external feedback. The repetition in this case is necessary, but even then it can backfire.

Your artificially relaxed state during blocked practice often leads to superior short-term performances. This has great potential to fool you and your golf instructors. How many times have you hit well on the practice tee, or in the presence of your instructor, only to have your confidence fly out the window when you actually play a round of golf? While limited blocked practice may help you get the feel of a new swing technique, it is as far from simulating real golf as almost any practice routine that exists. Beating balls may, to some degree, help you learn a skill, but it simply does not rehearse real competitive play.

WINNING THE BATTLE WITHIN
PRACTICE DRILLS

The drills presented in the following pages will help you develop your inner game and trust the swing you have learned through repetitive, blocked practice. You'll undoubtedly like some of them more than others and I encourage you to modify them in any way that suits your game. Some of these practice drills are my own creations, and some have been created and modified by the professionals and amateurs with whom I've worked. Have fun with them and let your imaginative mind get totally involved.

Inner Game Drills

The Tension-free Drill

This is a favorite of many of my students. It is perhaps the best drill for switching the focus from mechanics and external feedback to one of trust and internal feedback.

The tension-free drill is best done with a partner, but you can easily do it on your own. One golfer hits five to ten shots from the practice tee. After each shot, the golfer who hit the ball tells his partner, who is acting as the coach, how much tension he felt in his swing. Choosing a number from a scale of one to ten does this—with the number one indicating a tension-filled swing and the number ten, a tension-free one. Be careful not to confuse a lackadaisical approach with a tension-free one. A tension-free swing can be performed with a constant or even fast rhythm. Notice, for example, how world-class sprinters run their fastest when they appear the most relaxed. As gold-medal winners stride into the last 10 meters, their faces appear relaxed, not strained. What defines a tension-free swing is the amount of trust you have in it. A tension-free swing, one that finds its path of least resistance, almost inevitably results in your best golf shot. Conversely, a tension-filled swing will usually result in a mis-hit shot.

In *Tension Free Golf,* Dean Reinmuth further describes tension-free swings: "If you're overly concerned with adhering to the structure of what a good swing should look like, you'll rob yourself of the freedom and creativity that allow you to relax and make a free-flowing, rhythmic swing. For you to hit your best shots, the club head must flow smoothly, nonstop, from the start of the forward swing to the top of the finish, without the slightest hesitation, interruption, surge, jerk, or pull."

In an unrestricted golf swing, there will be tension in the muscles used to create the swinging motion, but the antagonistic muscles will be relaxed. By analogy, when executing a curl in weight training, the biceps contracts at the same time the triceps, the antagonistic muscle, relaxes. That action is tension-free and is the most powerful lifting mode. Tense triceps inhibits lifting power. A biomechanical expert could tell you which muscles are contracted during a golf swing, but the anatomy test we want you to pass is internally based. Allow the innate wisdom of your body and mind to find the tension-free swing path.

If this is a two-player drill, the golfer who is watching should be careful not to judge—by compliment or criticism—any shot made by the hitting partner. It's tempting to make some kind of judgment, especially through complimenting your partner on a good shot. You must not succumb to the temptation of encouraging your partner in this drill. Withholding judgment is critical because compliments and criticisms are external feedback. This drill is about getting players in touch with their own internal feedback systems, as a result of the movement, thus the first response must come from the player hitting the ball.

After each shot, before either player says anything, the player who hit the ball should immediately tap into his internal-feedback information bank and determine how much tension he felt during the swing. A major benefit of the drill is to learn to grab all of the information you can from within. At most, the player who is watching should ask questions like, "What number would you give that one?" or "How did that feel?" A player who fails to quickly evaluate the shot with a one-to-ten number is probably slipping into a mechanical judgment of the swing. Therefore, the question can jolt the hitter back into the internal evaluative mode. You should remind each other of the rules of the drill, if one of you begins to judge the other's performance. If your partner is having difficulty feeling the number of a swing, try using this question: "How did that swing compare to your previous one?" Or ask, "Was that swing freer or less free than the one before it?" Questions like these oblige the hitting player to reference internal-feedback information.

After the first player has finished hitting and evaluating several shots (five is a good number) on the 'tension meter,' the other player then hits an equal number of balls, and a similar series of shot-by-shot evaluations should take place. This drill will help you learn to trust your swing and develop your internal-feedback system. Learning to determine whether or not your swing was tension-free will help you with post-shot evaluations.

Your Next Shot Can Always Be a Ten

Michael, my co-author, loves this drill so much that he takes it onto the course with him and uses it even during competitive matches. He says focusing on swinging tension-free helps him eliminate the mechanical-swing thoughts that rob him of trust and rhythm. "The great thing about the game of golf is that your next swing can always be a ten," Michael says. "Of course, it's difficult to swing completely tension-free every time, but I've found that if you aim for a ten and don't make it, even a seven keeps you in the fairway, and you're still in the game."

This drill works even if you don't have a partner. It's a matter of disciplining yourself not to judge your shot or think about mechanics. (The more you do the drill, the easier and more fun it gets.) No matter how you hit your previous shot, you should strive to remain in the present, concentrating on allowing a tension-free swing on your next shot. This drill, beyond all the others, will prove to you that when you swing tension-free, you give yourself the best chance to hit a fine golf shot.

Murphy, in *The Kingdom of Shivas Irons,* says it this way: "The shot I just hit demands time for enjoyment. I savor the feeling of it. It became increasingly evident that simple, restorative attention develops with practice, growing stronger with repetition. We practice such awareness as we practice golf or other skills, and then we store something away for times when our thoughts and feelings wander." Through this development of internal-feedback awareness, by using inner-game drills, we arm our pre-shot routines with imagination and the possibility of trusting swings.

Low Energy and Full Release

This is Jeff Brehaut's favorite drill. "Because I'm swinging so slowly, it allows me to magnify the feel of the moves I may be working on," says Jeff. "It's good for rhythm, and it's great for your feel, to release the club fully while swinging slowly."

The drill is intended to familiarize you with the synchronization of your swing. Take a club—let's say a five iron—and aim at a target that is about 75 percent of your normal five iron distance. Obviously, you can hit the ball beyond this target with a five iron, but in this drill, I don't want you to. Take a full swing, and then hit the ball, making sure you finish the swing completely. It should appear as though you have just made a full swing, but in slow motion.

You'll be surprised at how completely you'll feel your club throughout this slow-motion swing. You'll get to know, kinesthetically, where the club head is at all times, and you'll become more accustomed to the feel of the shot. At first, many players have difficulty keeping the ball on line, but the drill is designed to allow the player to experiment with gauging the correct rhythm and tempo that allows the swing to come in on the beat and keep the ball on line. Even higher-handicap players eventually discover the swing synchronization that will send the ball on target.

This drill is harder than it might appear. Try, for example, hitting a driver only 100 yards with a full swing. Most players think they've throttled it down, and they still hit it 200 yards or more. Some higher handicappers are amazed at how far the ball goes with such little apparent effort. Reduce the club-head speed until you can hit the ball with your driver—with a full swing—to the 100-yard marker. Once that feel is established, hit it to 150 yards, and then to 200, each time concentrating on the feel of the full swing. You'll be pleasantly surprised at how in tune with your swing you will become. Some of my students have found it effective to reverse the order of the target yardage, starting at 200 yards and working down to 100.

Eyes Closed

This is Nick Ushijima's favorite drill. "I like them all and I use them all, but I especially like this one, because it completely allows my subconscious to take over," Nick says. "It allows me to be completely in my imaginative mind."

This is an enlightening drill for many golfers. Take your stance with your eyes open, then just before taking the club away from the ball, close your eyes. It is an amazing feeling, much like the old game of closing your eyes and falling backward into someone's arms. Without trust, you can't do it. If you don't trust your swing, just taking the club away from the ball is difficult. Stay with it, though. You'll get the hang of it, and you'll be surprised at how well you can hit the ball when you have total trust in your swing. This routine is structured to generate internal feedback that will link you directly to the feel of your swing. You'll feel it and perhaps even see it in your mind's eye. When students at my workshops are apprehensive about their abilities to swing and hit the ball with their eyes closed, I remind them that blind golfers learn to play quite well. After that sinks in, eyes-closed trust comes in two or three more swings.

McCarron told me that he and his caddie, Rich Mayo, had modified this drill. "I only shut my eyes at impact, instead of throughout the entire swing," McCarron says. "It still forces me to trust my swing, but I think I get clearer and more precise internal feedback about how the club head feels as it releases through the impact zone. Although the routes that swings take to eventually get to impact are varied, getting there with a tension free release, is essential I often use this drill when I'm warming up for a tournament. It's great for getting connected to your swing, and surprisingly, to the target."

Target Retention and the Imaginative Eye

This little mind-bender really works, when you can gather the discipline to employ it. The idea is for you to picture a target—let's say, a yellow flag 150 yards away—and hit whatever club gets you there. You should focus on the target, the path of the ball and imagine exactly where you want the ball to land.

Once you have the exact spot in mind, keep that mental image while you set up over the ball and take your swing. Throughout the swing—from the takeaway to the top of the backswing and down through the impact zone—the image of your ball landing on an exact spot should remain foremost in your imaginative mind. When you finish your swing, look up and focus on the spot you have chosen. The drill releases you from mechanical-swing thoughts during your swing and directly connects you to the target. This method of target-focus practice is an initial step toward inclusion of target and ball flight retention in your pre-shot routine.

One word of caution, though. This drill isn't easy to do. We are so accustomed to allowing mechanical-swing thoughts to infiltrate our brains during our swings that at first it will feel unnatural to concentrate solely on the target. But, once you get the feel of it, you will be surprised at how many of your shots actually land on or near your target.

Let it Go!

Arrange five to ten balls in a row so you can hit them in quick succession. The idea is to hit one shot, then immediately set up and hit the next one. You should be in almost perpetual motion until all the balls are hit, but you should come to a stop and address each shot. This is the drill that Eric, our long-drive champion, was illustrating in the story at the beginning of the chapter.

As Eric learned, this drill focuses you on the rhythm of your swing and on the target. Because the swings are in rapid succession, there is little time to judge your previous shot or to allow conscious swing thoughts to intrude. It's great fun with a driver, although it usually works well with any club.

Contingency Practice—Preparing for Competition

Earlier, I explained the importance of contingency practice. What follows are some innovative practice routines that will help you simulate an actual competitive golf round. They are the result of long conversations with such progressive golf professionals (swing coaches) as Laird Small of Pebble Beach Golf Academy; Tommy Masters of San Joaquin Country Club; Jim Toal of Spring Creek Country Club; Rod Souza of Stockton Country Club; Mitch Lowe of Del Rio Country Club; Val Verhunce of Adobe Creek; Eric Pollard of Ancil Hoffman; highly successful coaches in other sports (such as Walsh and Carroll), and a number of applied sport psychologists.

The drills consist of random and variable practice patterns designed to be golf's form of contingency and simulated practice. Pete Carroll uses these on 'competition Tuesday,' when every drill simulates game-time speed and execution. In golf competition, unless you are playing with some forgiving playing partners, no repeated swings are allowed. By emphasizing a one-shot-at-a-time premise, contingency practice allows enhanced learning and memory function. This leads directly to better performances during competition. The results of contingency practice are the opposite of those of overused blocked practice. Based upon my experience with the pros, performance during contingency practice may actually decrease, but performance during competition will increase. Overuse of blocked practice can lead to the opposite result.

Full Routine Practice

While practicing, always include some drills that consist of complete pre-shot and post-shot routines. Unless you practice your pre-shot and post-shot routines, they won't be automatic when you are actually playing. The more you rehearse the entire process, the more comfortable it will become. Performing your pre-shot and post-shot routines each time requires discipline, and you need to practice them so you will be prepared to execute them for eighteen competitive holes. Although some tour players use abbreviated routines, I believe even the world's highest-ranked players should use full-concentration practice. Here are some great contingency-practice drills you might want to try. These are called 'random-practice' drills.

Call Your Shot

In this drill, you call the next shot for your partner. The command should be specific, such as, "Okay, now hit a low draw that goes 175 yards." You can call for a high fade, a straight drive, a high-flop wedge, or any other shot you can think up for your partner to hit. Try not to request the same shot twice. You can do this one by yourself, of course, but be sure to hit a variety of shots and clubs. There are no repeats, much like competition; you must resist the temptation of rolling another ball over after a miss.

Sometimes players forget that golfers must react to the target, like in tennis or baseball, even though the golf ball is not moving toward them. This drill helps you react quickly, which keeps you in the moment with little time for conscious thought. For those of you who have not mastered a variety of shot-making skills, randomly changing targets, distances, and clubs for each shot will provide enough variety to make the drill challenging and worthwhile.

The drill also helps you rehearse situations on the course that call for creative shots. For example, you may find your ball in a divot or buried in a bunker. Or you may have a tree in a direct line to the pin. How will you react? How are you going to hit it? In most cases, you have choices and not much time to consider each one. Using this drill allows you to practice making quick decisions so that, in a real competitive round, you will be prepared for anything. As Bill Walsh so often has said, "If you are surprised by any situation during competition, you are not prepared."

Breath and Swing

This is a favorite drill of Triplett's. The goal is to learn to quiet your mind by using a deep, yogic breath that engages the diaphragm. Typically, the breath is inhaled -when Kirk takes his last look at the target and exhaled just before starting the swing. The breath does two things. It returns the player to present centeredness and relieves tension. Kirk says that when he breathes in this way his sense perceptions are heightened, he feels his center of gravity settle, and any tension escapes through the tips of his fingers and the soles of his feet. In this state, tension-free swings are easier to come by. With the breath, the conscious mind is quieted, and the imaginative mind is activated. As is the case with all inner game drills, tension-free levels are reported to your partner and to your internal feedback system after each swing.

Playing the Course

This is something you might want to use every time you practice. Visualize your favorite course or perhaps the next one you are going to play in competition, and play it in your mind. Hit every shot on a given hole until the ball makes the green, and then move on to the next tee. In your imagination, start on the first tee and move through five or six holes. If you are playing in a shotgun and will be starting your round on a difficult hole, begin there. You can also 'play' the final holes, imagining yourself coming down the stretch, battling for the lead. Visualize the course, the shots, your posture, and self-talk. And don't forget to use your full pre-shot and post-shot routines.

The benefits of this type of contingency practice are plentiful. Your imaginative mind is activated before you step onto the tee. While savoring each shot, you can react calmly to challenges. Doing this will make you more likely to stay in the present, enjoy the round, and, of course, shoot lower scores.

Aiming

This is a great one to do with a partner. Using your full pre-shot routine, walk into your address position, set up to the ball, and then have your partner lay a club down so it touches the heels of both of your golf shoes. Because players' toes can be flared out at different angles, as much as 45 degrees for some, heels are a more accurate measure of the lower-body line. Have your partner lay another club at your ball position, pointing toward the target, parallel to the club behind your heels. Before you move out of your address position, your partner should hold a third club that touches both of your shoulders. Have your partner hold the club in position as you back out of your stance so you can get a clear line of sight along the clubs on the ground toward your target. It's also important to check the alignment of your hips in relation to your feet, by placing a club just above your buttocks. By looking at the relative positions of the club your partner is holding and those on the ground, you can tell instantly whether your body is aligned properly and whether your stance is open or closed. You can check the alignment of your feet by yourself, too, of course. The club at your ball position determines whether the club-face is square to the target.

It's always a good idea to have your caddie, coach, or partner check your alignment during your warm-up. If you find, during your S.A.T. Process, that your aim is off, pay special attention to it while you are setting up for the next shot.

Extended Rope

While in the address position, look down an imaginary rope that extends from the ball to the target. (Sometimes, during workshops, we place a long, red rope on the target line, starting at a point about 20 yards in front of the ball.) As your eyes move back to the ball, retain the image of the rope extending to the target. Practice hitting shots with that image in your mind. Take a vivid image of your rope to the course, and you will see and feel the ball striping the fairway. This tool helps move your dynamic, imaginative energy out in front of you toward the target.

Quiet Your Mind

This drill will help you exorcise judgment and conscious thought during your swing. Choose some words or phrases to be part of your pre-shot routine that describe how you want your swing to feel. Then repeat them during your swing, blocking out all other thoughts and images. You may hum your favorite song, if you like. The idea is for you to block out all conscious thought, so you can concentrate on feeling your shot. Typically, descriptions of your most graceful swings are the most effective action words or phrases. Most players develop their own library of action phrases.

By using the same action phrase during warm-up as you do on the course, you mentally tie your swing to the words. This is like an actor, as we discussed earlier, who learns lines and stage directions together in a synchronized way. The action phrase becomes a positive trigger for you to set your body in motion without conscious thought. I've included in the Appendix a list of action phrases that I've accumulated from pros and amateurs alike over the years. Add yours to the list.

Short-Game Drills

The next set of drills introduces what is called 'variable practice.' The same swing program is repeated with variations of distance and direction. For example, you can hit short wedge and iron shots at a variety of targets, changing the distance and direction for each repetition. These swings are all partial swings, much like short-iron play during competition. There are no repeats, and you should use your full pre-shot and post-shot routines. Remember, shots from 100 yards and closer represent the scoring shots of your game. As the pros know, these shots correlate directly with lower scores, so it makes sense to devote a high percentage of your practice time to them.

To become one of the most accurate players from 125 yards and in, Triplett designed a practice regimen that really works for him. He works on six distances, two for each wedge. The distances range, in ten-yard intervals, from 125 yards for a full pitching wedge to 75 yards for a partial-swing, lob wedge. Kirk executes at least ten repetitions at each distance, developing his own internal distance control for each ten-yard interval. Although some players grip down on the club to change distances, Kirk likes to stay with his normal grip and adjust the swing length and tempo for partial-swing distances. The drill becomes livelier when he changes the distance on each repetition and employs his full-concentration routine. TPC of Scottsdale has some well-worn practice areas where Kirk crafted his world-class wedge game. Charlie Wi does a variation of Triplett's drill by using 5-yard intervals and gripping down on the club for shorter distances.

3x3 Drill: Chipping, Lobbing, and Bunker Shots

Place four strings in parallel rows on the green. Each string should be about six feet long. Place them perpendicular to your line of sight and about four feet apart from each other. Hit three balls with different clubs, from three different lies, to the first target, which is the space between the first and second strings. Then hit to the second target (between the second and third strings), and then to the third (between the third and fourth strings).

This variable practice will prepare you for play on the course, where conditions will likely vary on each chip. The 3x3 drill lets you hit high, arching, lob shots that hit and spin back, bump and run ships, bunker shots, and even putts or chips with a utility club. You should imagine whatever contingencies you might face in a competitive round.

Up-and-Down Game

On the practice green or on the course, spread ten to twenty balls around the green in a variety of locations. Playing the ball as it lies in the grass, get each ball up and down—utilizing your full putting routine whenever necessary (when you haven't chipped to 'gimme' range)—before moving to the next one. This is a great competition game with a partner or a team. It's similar to the McCarron 40-20, up-and-down drill described earlier.

Around the World

For this drill, which was borrowed from noted sport psychologist David Cook, place four markers on the putting green, each about three feet from the hole. Then place four more markers in a circle with a larger radius, about four feet from the hole. Starting from one of the four markers on the outer ring, putt one ball from each marker around the circle, making sure you go through your entire pre-shot routine before each putt. You must execute the last putt with your eyes closed. You are allowed two opportunities to make each putt, but if you miss twice you must go back to the first marker and go 'around the world' again. You can make the drill more difficult by giving yourself only one opportunity to make each putt, or by increasing the putting distance or the number of markers around the circle. Keep score by recording the total number of putts.

This putting drill prepares you for critical short putts that can mean everything in a round. It allows you to internalize the auditory sensation of hearing the putts drop and managing your emotions near the end of the drill when the pressure is on. You should rehearse from different distances, angles, breaks, speeds, and grains on the putting surface.

Ladder Drill

This is another David-Cook drill. Find a slight-to-moderate slope on the practice green. Place five, four-foot-long strings on the green approximately 18-24 inches apart. The strings should be placed parallel to one another so they resemble a ladder. Place tees six feet from each of the two end strings. Using one ball, putt it into each space in sequence. Since there are five strings, there are four spaces. Starting at one of the tees, putt toward the space nearest you, which is space one, until the ball stops in that space. Then putt to spaces two, three, four, three, two, and one. Keep score by recording the total number of putts. When you've climbed up and down the 'ladder,' move to the tee on the other end and repeat the drill. This is a great way to practice mid-range lag putts, working primarily on controlling the speed of the ball.

Remember to Have Fun

Feel free to modify these drills in any way you want. (I've included a few more in the Appendix.) I highly recommend you try to have fun with them, because practice should be something you look forward to. You're more likely to spend time practicing if it's enjoyable, and you'll get more out of it. If you walk away from the practice tee feeling mentally tired, but exhilarated at the same time (because you know the time spent is going to pay big dividends on the course), then you've done it right.

Now that you have powered your inner game, let's head to the next chapters and talk in more detail about developing positive self-talk.

12

POSITIVE SELF-TALK

One of the most universal and obvious changes on the PGA TOUR in the past decade has been the players' increased understanding of the importance of positive self-talk. No two participants personify this change more than the two most dominant players on their respective tours, Annika Sorenstam and Tiger Woods. They both clearly understand that the way they describe their games—to themselves in interior dialogues and to those around them in exterior ones—has a profound affect on their confidence, trust levels, and ultimately on their ability to reach peak performance.

Positive self-talk isn't mumbo jumbo, and it isn't fake. It's one of the most powerful weapons you will ever have in your golf bag. As we learned in earlier chapters, it's an indispensable part of pre-shot and post-shot routines. If you want to improve and compete successfully at any level, you'd better make it a standard part of your game. You'll find that positive self-talk has a number of benefits. If you employ it properly, you'll play better, score better, feel better, have more fun, and make more friends among your playing partners. Positive self-talk helps you manage negative emotions and keeps you in a positive frame of mind. Perhaps most important, it allows you to take control of your reactions to all situations, including playing partners, weather, course conditions, etc.

Elite golfers have correctly come to the conclusion that they need to be their own best friends on the golf course. Confidence demands this. Every harsh word you call yourself, whether internally or externally, tears at your self-confidence and makes it harder to trust your swing. It also drains you of the energy you need to play your best and to maximize enjoyment.

Self-talk is Power

Later in this chapter, I provide some examples of how self-talk can aid in what psychologists call 'internal cognitive restructuring,' which is a direct way we can gain control over ourselves and our emotions. Right now, I want to illustrate how powerful positive self-talk can be in the external world of practice and competition.

Most of us, at one time or another end up being paired with players we don't particularly care to be around. They may be loud, obnoxious, negative, full of one-upmanship, or of disagreeable natures. One female professional I work with had a particularly tough time playing with women she didn't like on the LPGA TOUR. She came to me upset one day when she learned the pairings of her tournament, which was a very important event for her status on the Tour.

"Oh, I'm going to hate this," she fumed. "I have to play with that witch. You know I hate playing with her. I'm going to have trouble focusing."

We talked for a while about her feelings, and then we developed a strategy based on a positive approach. "What I would suggest," I said, "is that you walk right up to her on the first tee, shake her hand, and say, 'Let's have a great time and go out and make some birdies.' After that, you won't have to say much to her the rest of the day. You will have made your positive statement and included her in it. That defuses any negative emotion you might have, puts you in a positive light, and allows you to concentrate on your game."

She did exactly that and played a fine round that day. "It worked!" she excitedly told me afterwards. "Now I don't have to worry about playing with jerks anymore!"

Positive self-talk—whether internal or external—is a matter of choice. It's your option to use it or not. Without it, you have little control over yourself or those around you, and you are susceptible to being swamped by lingering anger and by mechanical-swing thoughts. Negative emotions usually take you directly out of the imaginative mind and into fussing and fuming over perceived failures in your swing. Negative self-talk also tears at your self-confidence and leads directly to storytelling. Usually, the more negative the self-talk, the more whopping the stories. You can choose to be confident, but you must realize that positive self-talk is a critical ingredient in creating that confidence.

Before I get into some examples of positive self-talk and positive action phrases, I want to emphasize that you should practice positive self-talk on the driving range as well as on the course. It's a critically important part of contingency practice. Get out of the habit of harshly judging your shots. Awareness is fine—"I hung on and hit that one to the right. Let's figure out what happened and make the necessary adjustment." Negative self-talk will plunge you into self-doubt and even self-pity. Although self-pity may have a temporary narcotic effect, we all know that in the long run it's destructive and a sure-fire killer of joy, excitement, and effective execution.

Restructuring Internal Messages

Cognitive restructuring is a psychological term for the process of taking self-defeating thoughts and changing them into self-enhancing ones. Remember that self-talk includes not only what you say out loud, but also the reflective thoughts you have that others never hear. Some of the players I work with keep their thoughts to themselves, but if these thoughts are negative, they can be just as destructive as self-defeating transgressions that are said out loud. You can change this habit not only in golf, but also in your daily life. You'll find the payoff to be enormous in the long run. There's an old saying that it isn't what happens to you in life that matters, but rather how you react to it. I would add that in the golfing world, the way you react to what happens to you is what determines your success on the course. It defines you as a player. Improvement lies in the process of positive cognitive restructuring, and self-talk is a major part of that restructuring.

Positive self-talk comes in two categories. The first category includes supportive language, like: *you can do it; hang in there; you have the game, etc.* The second category is comprised of task-specific instructions, such as: *get back to the target; take a breath; feel your swing; be aware of your tempo; release it; stay in the present, etc.*

Here are some other examples of positive-self-talk choices you can make when it comes to golf. I have adapted them to golf from a cognitive-restructuring program developed by Linda Buckner at the University of Virginia. Note that the most powerful, self-enhancing thoughts are expressed in the first person, present tense. I am sure you will find some of these phrases familiar.

Self-defeating thoughts:	Self-enhancing thoughts:
Another horrible shot. Why am I such a jerk?	*I hit that one to the right. Big deal. I'm replacing that swing feel with a tension-free one.*

What a terrible bounce! I never get a break!

If that's the worst thing that happens to me in this round, it's going to be a good day. I am hitting this next shot with a trusting swing.

I hate four footers! I'm going to choke!

I'm making this putt because I've practiced it a hundred times. I'll execute the process and let the outcome take care of itself.

I'm an idiot with no talent. I shouldn't be golfing.

The great thing about golf is that my next swing can always be a ten. I learn something every time I play.

Wouldn't you know it! It's raining. I hate rain!

Great! It's raining! I am prepared and I like playing in the rain. It gives me an advantage over all the other players who don't like it.

My swing is terrible. Everybody knows it.

There is no such thing as the perfect swing. I trust the swing I have and will play well.

With my slice, I'm sure to end up in the lake. (Shrug)

I don't bother with outcomes. I use my routine, commit to my strategy, focus on my target, see the shot in my mind, and trust my swing. That's all that is required of me.

I can't play in these conditions!	*Great! The conditions are tough. I like it that way. It gives me an advantage over the other golfers who won't like these conditions.*
Wouldn't you know it! I have to play with jerks.	*Let me take control. I am positive; I wish them luck; then I forget about them, and I play my own game.*
I'm scared. I will fail today.	*Hey, it's all an adventure. If I have fun, focus on my routines, and learn something, it will be a good day.*
My partner or caddie gave me the wrong yardage!	*No big deal. It was my fault for not checking the yardage myself. I'll pull this next shot off and make us both feel better.*
I don't feel like playing golf today. I should be working.	*I'm here golfing, and as long as I am, I'm going to make it the most important thing in the world that I can be doing right now. I'll work when I work.*
I can't hit the ball. It's my coach's fault!	*I trust my coach, and I know I'm on the right track. My game is ultimately my own responsibility. I'll work on it today and ask questions tomorrow.*

Blow this shot, dummy, and you'll ruin your good drive.

No previous shot matters. Only this one does. I'll just execute my routine, and everything will be okay.

I just can't keep up with these young players.

I'm experienced and I know how to practice and maximize my strengths.

Action Phrases

Many elite players use action phrases to help connect their imaginations with the movement of the golf swing. That's a sport psychologist's way of saying they use action phrases to put themselves in a positive frame of mind. These phrases or words typically emerge from their best performance swings and relate to tempo, rhythm, and whole-swing movements. It's similar to what skilled writers do with words. They take concepts and weave them into smooth, elegant sentences, paragraphs and pages in the same way elite golfers meld swing positions into flowing, graceful swings. We play our best when our swing sentences form creative paragraphs. Action phrases help players 'see' and 'feel' the game. They also act as positive reinforcement and help golfers create a comfort and trust zone for the day.

McCarron has asked many players on the PGA TOUR about action phrases, and most say they use them regularly. When Scott was a rookie, he played with Tom Kite, who introduced him to the concept. Kite repeats the same action phrase to himself throughout an entire four-day tournament, if he is playing well.

Triplett likes 'see, feel and trust' as his three-step mantra. Wi likes to say "see the picture (of his swing) and the target' (connecting the picture to the intended ball flight and target).

Action phrases are not conscious swing thoughts; rather, they take the place of swing thoughts by describing some aspect of the swing and then connecting it to the whole. You might want to pick one from this list as your action phrase for your next round, or better yet, create your own. I recommend that you develop your own list of phrases from descriptions of your most trusting swings.

Tempo	Release	Target
Rhythm	Free it up	Release
Aim	Go	
Swing freely	See the target	
Feel	Be aggressive	
Smooth	Finish	
Slow	Full throttle	
Trust	See the line	

A Worthwhile Goal

Positive self-talk isn't as easy as it might seem, at first. Staying positive and focused on the task at hand requires discipline and practice. You can start by training yourself to say only positive things about your shot or your ball. Don't cuss at it, belittle it, make fun of it, or yell things like, "Go ahead you rotten thing, get into the woods! That's where you belong!"

This may seem funny when you see it on paper, but how often do you hear golfers say things like that? Unfortunately, most of us hear such negative talk on a frequent basis. Positive self-talk is critically important to improving your game. It takes a little work, at first, to get into the habit of using positive self-talk on the course, but it is well worth the effort. Nearly every professional will tell you that it is definitely a worthwhile goal. Ultimately, the greatest thing you can realize about positive self-talk is that it gives you control over yourself and your game. By developing and practicing your personal arsenal of positive self-talk, you can learn to be as good at it as the top players on the PGA TOUR—and they are all pretty good at it. They fully understand that staying positive is a critical step in permanent improvement, and a powerful key that helps open the door to the winner's circle.

13

BUILDING YOUR
PRE-SHOT ROUTINE

I'm not going to spend a great deal of time on pre-shot routines, because much has already been written about them in numerous other publications. Even so, it is clear to me that most amateurs don't quite understand how critical a good pre-shot routine is to their games. Ultimately, a successful pre-shot routine occupies your conscious thoughts and puts you into a positive and imaginative frame of mind just before you hit your shot. It does a number of other positive things, as well, and acts as a source of confidence and trust. If you are wondering whether you should go to the trouble of building a pre-shot routine, here's a fact that should motivate you—virtually all professional golfers on the various tours, and elite amateurs as well, use some version of a pre-shot routine. On the other hand, very few mid-to-high handicappers have pre-shot routines that they use consistently. So, it's more than just a cool thing to do. A good pre-shot routine really works. Once you develop one you like, you won't feel comfortable playing without it.

Practice Your Routine

Before we get into the anatomy of a good pre-shot routine, I want to remind you that in order to integrate it into your game properly, you should practice it whenever you hit range balls. Some players might find it strange to practice a pre-shot routine, but repetition is critical if you are going to make one an automatic part of your game. Unless you are conducting one of the special drills I outlined earlier, I highly recommend you conduct your pre-shot routine each time you hit a practice ball. This is critical because executing your pre-shot routine on the course can be a distraction, unless you've rehearsed it on the practice tee. Building your pre-shot routine, especially at first, requires conscious thought and focus. As with learning any new technique, you'll have to repeat it many times before it becomes comfortable and automatic. This repetition should first take place on the practice range.

Because they have committed their pre-shot routines to long-term memory through diligent preparation, some professionals and elite amateurs use abbreviated routines during practice. They are still careful, however, to step into their address positions from the side, as they would with their full routines, taking the same amount of time and using the same number of looks at the target, waggles, and imaging. You probably already have a consistent way you walk into each shot, but you may not be so consistent with the rest of the routine, such as committing to a strategy, aligning your body, aiming in your mind, using imagery, and trusting your swing.

Pre-shot routines vary from player to player, but in general, they are simply a repeated process through which players prepare themselves mentally and physically to hit their best possible shots.

Precise and Repeatable

At the 2005 AT&T National Pro-Am at Pebble Beach, I had a chance to watch one of my students, Charlie Wi, play a practice round with his idol, K.J. Choi. Although he had been highly successful on the Japanese and Asian tours, Charlie was a rookie on the PGA TOUR at the time. Choi, of course, was a toughened PGA veteran who routinely battled for leads in major tournaments. It was instructive to watch both players' pre-shot routines. It also explained to me just why Choi is one of golf's best ball-strikers.

As the day went on, I noticed that Charlie's pre-shot routine varied slightly from shot to shot. He didn't take the same amount of time before each shot, and his routine wasn't as precise as usual. At times, he did not appear to be settled in when he took his club back. These were never his best shots; in fact, most of them were mis-hit to some degree. I was a little surprised by the inconsistency in Charlie's pre-shot routine. We had worked together many times, and I knew he had an established routine, but for some reason, he was a little off that day.

At the same time, Choi repeated his pre-shot routine with amazing, machine-like precision. He always took exactly the same amount of time, and he looked completely relaxed by the time he took the club away. You could almost see the clarity in his mind when he finished his routine. It was perhaps the biggest difference I saw all day between the highly successful veteran and Charlie. After the round, Charlie and I talked about the inconsistency in his pre-shot routine, and within a short time, after a session on the range, he was back on track. He confided to me that during the practice round he had failed to commit to some of his strategies, experienced an occasional lazy-target focus, and lapsed into a mechanical-swing thought or two. He grew excited as he talked

about the improvements he was going to make in this area. Charlie
has a world-class game, and I had no doubt that he would be successful, as he proved last year by moving into the top 50 on the
PGA Tour.

Kenny G. and the Art of Chipping in Harmony

During the AT&T, Choi's amateur partner was the famous saxophon-
ist, Kenny G. Kenny is an engaging personality and a wonderful golfer
who usually carries a one handicap. I had a chance to talk to him during the round. He told me he had been a little frustrated with his game
of late, saying he was working with about ten swing thoughts.

"Only ten?" I asked, tongue-in-cheek.

"Well," said Kenny with a little grin. "I have about 100 more
in my swing-thought library." Our conversation then turned to the
musical concert that Kenny was going to give for the AT&T volun-
teers that week.

"What will you think about when you play your saxophone on
stage?" I asked.

"Nothing," he replied. "I don't think of anything at all when I play
music." He looked at me, realized where I was going with the question,
and shook his head. "I know what you're going to say, but I can't play
golf without thinking, because I haven't mastered the techniques."

I shook off his reasoning and asked if he had ever tried playing golf with the same mental attitude and approach that he used in
music. He admitted that he hadn't. He smiled when he said it
because again he knew where I was going. I suggested that he consider getting his swing thoughts down to just one the next time he
played. I told him that Dave Brubeck, the renowned jazz artist,
once told an audience at the University of the Pacific that although
musicians never know exactly where the music will flow during a
concert, they typically play in the manner that they practice.

Brubeck would say that simulating a concert in rehearsal is critical. I suggested to Kenny that he practice limiting his swing thoughts to one or none the next time he was on the range. I also told him that the swing he had would most likely be the one he would use in the tournament, so why not let it go just like he would the riffs he would captivate the crowd with at the concert.

Kenny then confided to me that he was having a terrible time with his chipping. He had the yips. His only recourse was to hood an eight iron when he chipped because wedges were pretty scary to him.

I asked him if he would try something for me. He laughed and nodded. I asked him to sing a middle C, which he did. I then asked him to hum the same note during his pre-shot routine before hitting a chip shot. He was to hum as he approached the ball and continue while he chipped. He grinned and tried it. To his surprise, he began chipping beautifully. The exercise did exactly what it was supposed to do—it quieted his conscious mind and allowed his imagination to kick in. He became comfortable and relaxed, with no thoughts of mechanics or negative outcomes.

Not all of you, of course, will be comfortable humming during your pre-shot routines, but you should customize your own pre-shot routine by including some activity that matches your personality and imagination, so that a trusting swing has chance to flow from it. Kenny enjoyed the lesson. I told him that I had instructed other players to hum while swinging during their pre-shot routines, but this was the first time I had ever seen a player with perfect pitch, pitch perfectly.

The Anatomy of a Pre-Shot Routine: Your S.A.T. Process Revisited

In many ways, your pre-shot routine and your S.A.T. Process (post-shot routine) are linked tightly together. One way to keep the synchronicity of the two is to use strategy, aim, and trust as the core of your pre-shot routine, as well. Here's how that can work.

Strategy

You should always be conscious of the strategy you choose and make sure you buy into it before you swing. Start your pre-shot routine by standing about 15 feet behind the ball looking over it toward the target. From this vantage point, you can see the entire flight of your shot in your mind's eye. At this time, you should process all conscious information—the lie of the ball, the wind direction, where the dangers are located (lake on the left, for example), and all other information of that nature. This takes only a couple of seconds as you decide your strategy for the shot. The time it takes you to determine strategy, of course, depends upon your familiarity with the course and existing strategic variables like wind, uphill and downhill lies, hazards, etc.

It is critical, at this point, that you commit to and take full responsibility for your strategy. That means a total commitment to this shot, at this specific moment. It is amazing how often golfers do not fully buy in to their own strategies. This is the time to be fully conscious and aware of the strategy you choose. If you choose to hit a hard six iron instead of a soft five, then affirm that the six is your best choice. Picture exactly where the ball will land, and then 'feel' the swing that will get the ball to that spot. Consciously buying in to your strategy allows you to trust your swing. Be sure to select a strategy that fits your game and the situation. If you prefer to play the ball left to right, as McCarron does, don't attempt to draw a five iron in to a tight left pin. Take a conservative line, like the center of the green, and make an aggressive play.

This is also the time to acknowledge any fears or doubts about the upcoming shot. If there is a ball-grabbing lake on the left, for example, you may be harboring a negative mental picture of plunking one into the middle of it. Acknowledge that fear, replace it with the thought that plunking one into the lake simply isn't relevant, and get back to the visual image of the target and the shot you planned. It's too much to ask yourself to never have negative thoughts, like hitting one into the lake, but you can ensure that the last thing in your mind is a positive image of the target you've selected. Don't worry about the outcome of the shot; your only concern is about executing the process. In the back of your mind, you should be comforted by the knowledge that only a complete breakdown of your process will cause a mis-hit to occur.

Acknowledge the hazard and your fear of hitting into it, and then simply say to yourself, "All I have to do is lock into a target and execute the swing process, and the ball flight will take care of itself." Rarely will your ball fly into trouble, if you take the tension out of your swing in this manner. As Pete Carroll says, use the power of attraction rather then distraction.

The Magical Moment

The next step is the one that makes golf truly magical. Once you've chosen and committed to a strategy, a *trigger* helps make the transfer from the conscious, decision-making mind to the unconscious mind of imagination—from conscious strategy to feeling the right swing. You can use any number of triggers. McCarron tugs on his glove just before he moves toward the ball. Some players trigger the transition by twirling the club in one hand; others shift the club from one hand to the other. Whatever your trigger, make it comfortable, so you can repeat it each time you approach the ball. Sport psychologist, Dick Coop, feels that if the trigger is not changed periodically (every two to three weeks), it can become part of a ritual and won't cleanly facilitate the conscious-mind-to-imaginative-mind transfer. It's a good idea, then, to have more than one trigger.

Your approach to the ball should match your personality. If you are an aggressive player like Nick Price or Tiger Woods, your approach should be aggressive and done with some speed, but never rushed. Or you may be more deliberate, like Ernie Els or Phil Mickelson, who approach the ball more slowly. Choose whatever approach is right for you.

By now, you should be free of your conscious mind. Do not analyze your previous shots to determine whether you will hit this one correctly. You should not second-guess your strategy, and you should be aware of any negative emotions that emerge. There is no rule in golf that says you can't stop your routine and start over, so if you feel any negative emotions at this point, back away, change them and begin again. Remember, Murphy says that golf is a game of seeing and feeling, so make sure you have managed your emotions and have made the shift to your imagination.

Aim

As you settle into your stance, take care to align your feet, hips, and shoulders to accommodate the shot you see. Because you have practiced settling into your address position many times, you will be able to do so without conscious thought. Many players pick out something in the turf, such as a tee, a tuft of grass, or a leaf a few inches ahead of the ball and in line with the target and the face of the club. Then they imagine a pathway from the ball through the marker on an imaginary path to the target. This helps with alignment. Golf books, magazine articles, and Golf-Channel-Academy-Live broadcasts describe the parallel-left alignment as 'square.' Imagine two railroad tracks extending to infinity with your body aligned to the left track and the ball on the right one aligned to the target. Parallel left, or square, is not necessarily the most efficient alignment for everyone, but you should start with parallel left, find out what is best for you, and then practice it. For example, McCarron has found that aiming his lower body at the target line is best for him. Fred Couples may be aligned as far as 20 yards left, or open. With his engineering background, Triplett describes his body and target lines as vectors with length representing the magnitude, and orientation in space representing the direction. This is a powerful aiming combination for him. While you are aligning your body and clubface, project your imagination (vectors) toward the target. Retaining the image of the shot and feeling the swing that matches what you see are products of an effective pre-shot routine. Retaining the image of the shot and feeling the swing that matches what you see are products of an effective pre-shot routine.

Trust

Now that we have established the strategy and aiming portions of the pre-shot routine, it's time to trust your swing. Once over the ball, you may need another trigger to initiate the swing. Some players still use a waggle. I recommend a deep, cleansing breath that allows you to move into the more profound and imaginative phase of the pre-shot routine. The Zen masters tell us that a cleansing breath creates present centeredness, relieves tension, and helps bring emotion into balance. Then visualization and kinesthetic awareness take over as your imagination is activated, mechanical-swing thoughts fall away, and you completely enter the imaginative mind—seeing and feeling the upcoming swing. While keeping the target in your mind's eye, initiate the swing you sensed in advance.

That is trust—the magical feeling of hitting a 'ten' on the tension-free meter by letting go and swinging without conscious thought. It's one of the reasons golfers continue to golf. Using a pre-shot routine does not guarantee perfect execution, but it does guarantee that you give yourself the best chance to trust the swing you have. It's a great way to systematically use your conscious mind to develop strategy, transition into your imaginative mind to gain the feel of the shot you see, and focus on the target for a trusting swing. You'll be surprised at the progress you will make toward consistently clearing your mind by practicing and repeating your pre-shot routine. A calm, focused mind within each pre-shot routine creates opportunities for graceful swings.

Michael Murphy sums it up this way: "To clear your mind before each shot, to learn from each failure and success, to bring kinesthetic imagination to the swing, and to constantly reclaim the future of the moment."

14

KEEPING A SPORT JOURNAL

One thing I highly recommend to all golfers is to keep a sport journal. I know that some people are not comfortable with writing, but just remember, your journal doesn't have to be *War and Peace.* In fact, the simpler and more natural the writing, the better. The easiest way to get something down on paper is to pretend you are talking to a friend and write down exactly what you would say. We speak hundreds of thousands more words in a lifetime than we write, so speaking generally comes easier and more naturally. You'll find that 'speaking' the words into your journal is not hard to do.

Keeping a sport journal has a number of benefits. First and foremost, it helps you gain insight into the mental processes that determine the quality of your golf. It also gives you an opportunity to record the different strategies you use to maintain a best-performance state and the intervention strategies you use to regain control. The long-range goal is to help you develop and record the techniques to implement in stressful situations.

The journal is also a great place to record your feelings and the inner, personal knowledge you gain related to performance. It is beneficial to express these feelings in such a way that you remember them and can better understand them. You should record your anxiety about or confidence in certain shots, how you dealt with it, and what outcomes were achieved. You can identify positives and negatives in this way, and you can begin to implement the positives on a more regular basis.

You don't have to make a journal entry every day, but you should date the entries you do make. The journal is an informal record of your thoughts and experiences as you train for and maintain high-level performances. Letting someone you trust review your journal can be highly beneficial. They should use it to guide you into further self discoveries.

What to Include in Your Journal

Sport psychologist, Ken Ravizza, has developed a sport-competition-journal guideline that I have made specific to golf. Here are a few guidelines you can use:

1. Peak Performance State—What does it feel like (attitude, motivation, and emotion) when you play and practice at your best?

2. Stresses Away From the Course—Write down your thoughts about events at work, home, or school that are distracting you. You can also list the on-course distractions that might include your playing partners, noise, weather, or poor equipment.

3. Teachers and Coaches—What do you need from them? Are there parts of your game that you feel you need help to strengthen? What can you do to make your relationships with your teachers and coaches more productive?

4. Confidence—On a scale of one to ten, how was your confidence level today? Why? Do you feel confidence is a matter of choice? What can you do differently to feel more confident?

5. Awareness and Concentration—What changes did you observe in your performance when you were totally aware and present versus when you were distracted? What concentration methods are you using? Are they working?

6. Stress—How and when did you feel anxious during the round? How did that stress manifest itself? This is a hard question and usually requires a little soul-searching, so be sure to reward yourself with something you like when you give a truthful answer here. How did you handle the stress? Was that successful?

7. Relaxation Training—How are your relaxation skills developing? What method works best for you? Are you able to relate this to your play?

8. Self-Talk—Did you successfully 'talk' your way through the round, staying positive and thinking like Annika, Tiger, Jack, and Phil? Or, did you call yourself names and fall into negative traps? If you did, that's okay. The beautiful thing about golf is you can always tee it up again tomorrow!

9. Imagery—How are your imagery skills developing? Do you see the ball flight on the movie screen in your head, or is it more of a feeling image? Or both? At what point do you notice lapses in imagery? How clear are your images? Can you control the speed and tempo of the image?

10. Pressure Situations—How are you handling pressure situations? What works and what doesn't? How will you prepare for the next pressure shot?

11. Quality Practice Time—Are you preparing mentally for practice? Did you feel you had a good practice? Why? A poor practice? Why? How can you better prepare next time?

Excerpts from Scott's Journal

McCarron does a great job of keeping a sport journal, and I know he not only enjoys it, but he also finds it an extremely helpful tool. He graciously allowed me to use the following excerpts. You might note that he writes freely about both technique and his mental attitudes and approaches.

> After my third round at the Hope (The Bob Hope Classic in Palm Springs, California) I went back to reading an old entry in this journal, made when I was playing and putting really well. I was reminded that I had great success lining up the words on the ball straight down the putting line, and squaring up the mid-line mark on my putter with those words. On the fourth day of the Hope, I decided to try this key again. I ended up birdying the first four holes. I shot a 65 to go to ten under par and easily make the cut. I had a bogey-free round on Sunday and went to 14 under.

Other excerpts from Scott's journal include:

> The one negative thought that interferes with my ability to attain my ideal mental state is the fear that I will fail to meet my expectations.

> As I enter my ideal competitive mental state, my behavior and attitude definitely change. I become more focused. I'm really only aware of my task at hand and going through my routine. I'm not bothered by noises or other things going on around me.

During the round (Scott shot in the sixties the day he wrote this), I was focused on seeing the fairways and greens very vividly. I wasn't seeing the trouble.

When I play badly, I try to figure out why after the round. I get angry and frustrated when I can't figure out why I wasted shots. Usually, however, I can trace swing and shot-making mis-hits to a fast routine or lack of full concentration on my target.

I played well today, because I concentrated on my routine and positive self-talk.

When negative thoughts came into my head, I thought one shot at a time, and then took a deep breath and exhaled.

While over a shot, any shot, I think, 'see, feel, trust'—see the target, feel the swing that matches what you see, and trust what you see and feel.

I finally figured out that I don't have to make dramatic swing changes to be a winner. I just have to believe in myself.

Over the course of your golfing career, this kind of feedback can be enlightening and self-instructive. The data that an open, reflective, and aware golfer like Scott can produce in a sport journal is quite powerful.

Keeping a sport journal may seem a bit odd to those of you not accustomed to writing, but you'll be surprised at how fun and educational it can be. You'll probably find, as McCarron did, that by reviewing your entries from months or even years before, you'll find tips that can immediately help your game today. The past can be a great teacher, if we will just pay attention. Since memories are notoriously short when it comes to golf, it really helps to write things down. You'll be surprised at how much fun you'll have reading your sport journal, once you've made a habit of keeping it.

15

TAKING IT TO THE COURSE

Most golfers will agree that the walk from the practice tee to the first tee is a long and difficult one often fraught with anxiety and fear. Contingency and inner-game practice will help you gain confidence in your game and trust in your swing. With discipline and dedicated practice, using drills presented earlier (especially the ones that involve exercising your imaginative mind), you can best prepare for taking your game to the course. As we all know, there is nothing quite like the excitement and challenge of actually teeing up in competition.

Unfortunately, for a surprisingly large number of players, the emotion they feel on the first tee is not positive. Too many golfers experience great fear and even dread, rather than feeling confidence and joy. This chapter is devoted to substituting the negative emotions that you may experience during competition with positive ones that will allow you to be more successful.

Negative emotions have a number of sources. Among them are:
- a sole focus on mechanical-swing thoughts,
- a lack of proper practice,
- a lack of belief in your instructors,

- a lack of pre-shot, in-between-shot and post-shot routines,
- storytelling while still on the course,
- negative self-talk,
- a focus on outcomes rather than on processes,
- waging bets that are too large,
- playing with lower-handicap golfers.

Facing Down the Demons

Everyone faces internal demons on the golf course. It is one of the unique elements that makes this game so fascinating. Even the top players in the world struggle with internal challenges on a weekly basis. The trick is to get to know your own demons and learn how to disarm and neutralize them. McCarron knows his demons, and he'll tell you that it is his preparation through quality practice that allows him to face them down.

As an example of the struggles that even an experienced professional golfer can go through in competition, I want to relate the story of an extraordinary tournament that Scott played at the Reno-Tahoe Open held near Lake Tahoe, Nevada, in 2004. During the tournament, which is a regular, PGA-TOUR stop, Scott faced and overcame several of the familiar fears that haunt most of us at some point during competitive rounds. How he handled these distractions is an intriguing tale that may give you some insight into how you, too, can overcome them during intense competition.

Playing Before Friends and Family

Because Scott lives in Reno, Nevada, near Montreux Golf and Country Club, where the Reno-Tahoe Open is held, a number of his friends and family members turned out to watch him play. The group included several old college and high school friends, and Scott felt extra pressure to perform well in front of them.

He had been playing well on the PGA TOUR coming into the event, but the stakes were high because he had yet to earn enough money to secure his playing privileges for the next year. He responded well early, shooting 69 and 67 the first two days, playing himself into contention. Suddenly, his mind-set changed from merely wanting to play well to thinking about winning the tournament. He got ahead of himself and early in the third round he found himself pressing and mis-hitting shots. He was also trying too hard in front of his hometown fans. As a result, he strayed from his normal routines and began to focus on mechanical-swing thoughts. As soon as he did, he began losing his concentration and 'feel,' and he stopped visualizing his shots. He related to me later that the game suddenly became more difficult. Frustration set in, and he began to lose patience. His pre-shot routines became shortened, and he seldom performed his post-shot routines. He was focusing on the outcome of the tournament and his score, rather than on the processes he had established for himself. In short, he stopped trusting his game. He made some bogeys and it appeared that any chance he had to win was blown away in the stiff Nevada winds. Then an unlikely event transpired that put him back on the right track. Montreux is a beautiful course tucked into the rugged shoulder of the Sierra Nevada just north of Lake Tahoe. The course has a fair amount of slope to it and Scott turned his ankle after playing his ball from the rough off the 9th fairway. It was a bad sprain and it hurt like hell. His ankle was swelling and felt as if it were on fire, but with everyone out to cheer him on, he didn't feel as if he could quit the field. Instead, he had his ankle taped at the turn, and he modified his swing to accommodate the fact that he couldn't put as much stress on it.

The new development had a surprising result. He suddenly began to swing by 'feel' in order to hit the ball with a minimum of pain. He began to get away from his mechanical-swing thoughts. This led to a greater visualization of his shots and thus he began to play in his imaginative mind, rather than through an attempt at mechanical manipulation. In effect, he began to 'let go to gain control.'

Scott's drives began finding the middle of the fairways and he started hitting high, soft irons close to the hole. He made some birdies and finished the day with a respectable 71.

The final day was windy, with gusts up to 35 miles per hour. Scott battled the swirling winds and his own nerves all day. He held on, performed his routines and trusted his swing. He played well, not knowing the other players were faltering in the fickle wind-storm. Then someone told him he was closing in on the lead. Despite his years of experience on the Tour, the realization that he had a chance to win changed his mental environment. He grew tight. His rhythm changed, his swing shortened, and he began to quicken his pre-shot and post-shot routines again. Pressure manifests itself in a variety of ways, and Scott, like many other golfers, tends to speed up his natural tempo under intense pressure. On the 16th hole, battling for the lead, he didn't trust his swing, hit his ball into a bunker, and bogeyed the hole. That dropped him two shots behind Taylor Vaughan, the tournament leader.

Number 17 at Montreux is a par five that McCarron, one of the longer hitters on the Tour, can usually expect to birdie. After hitting a monster, 390-yard drive (the ball flies about 10 percent farther than normal in the thin air at Lake Tahoe), he did not hit his usual quality golf shot into the green. He lost focus on his normal routines and didn't properly visualize and 'feel' his iron shots before he swung. He walked away with a disappointing par on the hole.

The final hole is a difficult par four and Scott found himself over the green on a downhill slope with a nearly impossible third shot.

He knew he had to get up and down to have any chance at a playoff. The final few holes had been nerve-wracking and his patience and confidence were ebbing. He gathered himself, took a deep breath, and vowed to concentrate fully on the procedures he had practiced so often. He carefully went through his pre-shot routine. He began to feel the confidence flowing back as he found the familiar mental keys he needed. "Just go through the process," he told himself. "You've hit this shot thousands of times. Just see it to the hole."

As he took his club back, Scott retained the mental picture of his ball ending up close to the hole. He trusted his swing, stayed in rhythm, and hit a beautiful shot. He made his putt for a superb par to finish at ten under for the tournament.

As it turned out, the other players, including Vaughan, also struggled in the wind down the stretch, and Scott ended up in a four-way playoff. Vaughan, who faced demons of his own after building a huge lead only to see it evaporate, refocused on his processes and made a pressure-packed putt to win the tournament. He, too, had begun to hurry his rhythm and swings as the pressure mounted, only to return to his imaginative mind and regain trust of his swing.

Scott finished second and earned enough prize money to keep his PGA-TOUR card. He also felt he learned some valuable lessons. "The fact is, golf isn't a static game," Scott said. "Pressure disappears and then reappears in different forms and it can catch you off guard at any moment. That's why your routines, your mental processes, staying in the present, and playing in your imaginative mind are so important. They are your armor against pressure and what it does to you. They are all you have out there. They provide you with trust and confidence."

Pressure Reducers

When you take your game from the practice tee to the course, you get to take only what you have practiced with you. (This is a very good message for Kenny G.) The preparation you've done through practice is as important as your clubs, shoes, balls, tees, and all your other equipment. Preparation is a tangible thing; few golfers can play quality, competitive golf without it.

As you stand on the first tee, learn to trust your preparation. Let your mind sweep back over the things you've been working on. Let the trust and confidence you've built up from your practice and your lessons fill you with positive energy and imagery.

Warming up Before Your Round

Warming up before you tee off should be more than an exercise to loosen your muscles—it should also loosen your imagination. Before you begin to hit practice balls, you should connect mentally to a target. As you are loosening up, swing your club down an imaginary line to a real target and feel the weight of the club head throughout. Focus your mind on the target and visualize your ball flying on a true line to it.

I recommend starting your warm-up with shorter shots. This gives your body a chance to loosen up and allows your mind to tap into target retention. But, you should do what works for you. Jeff Wilson, for example, who is one of the nation's best amateurs, likes to warm-up first with his driver to find his rhythm and then move on to other clubs.

As you move into your warm-up, be sure to practice your pre-shot routine each time, so you are into a full rhythm by the time you step onto the first tee. Practice the exact shots you are going to need on the first few holes, so you can see everything in your imaginative mind. Swing with rhythm and without tension. If there is a primary concentration point, it should be to groove your swing so you are swinging 8 to 10 on your tension-free, swing meter. Get in touch with how it feels to swing tension-free and maintain target retention as you swing. Practice a couple of fades and draws with the nine-ball-challenge drill, and if it's windy, make sure you get the feel of hitting the ball on a low trajectory. Swinging tension-free is the key, here, though. Early in your warm-up, use one or two of your favorite inner-game drills – eyes closed at impact, let it go, etc.

Toward the end of your warm-up, make sure you hit the club you plan to use on the first tee. Visualize the shot—go through your exact pre-shot routine and see the ball and your target clearly in your mind. Many of the top players with whom I work like to play the first three to five holes on the range at the end of their range-practice time.

On the putting green, it's best to use just one ball. Again, go through your pre-putting routine and see the ball, in your mind's eye, drop into the center of the cup. I recommend beginning with long putts (40 to 50 feet) so you get the feel of the long strokes and speed. Then practice some medium-distance putts (10 to 15 feet) and finally some short ones (three to four feet), keeping in your imaginative mind that these are for birdies and pars on the first few holes.

Course Management

It is a good rule of thumb that your course strategy should be conservative but that you should hit your shots aggressively. For competitive rounds, I highly recommend that you know exactly what shot you plan to hit off every tee before the round begins. Also, give some thought to the last couple of holes on the course. Imagine the end of the tournament and put yourself in the position of being one behind the leader with two holes to go. What clubs are you going to use on the last two holes? Don't write your victory speech yet, but visualize yourself leading the tournament. What clubs will you hit off the final two tees? Have your strategy firmly in mind before you set foot on the course. The last place you should design strategy is on the final few holes of a tournament when the pressure is on.

You should know your strengths as a golfer and always plan your course strategy around them. If you are a great driver of the ball, then you may want to be more aggressive off the tee. However, you also need the discipline to throttle down the 'Big Dog' on holes that are short and narrow. If iron play is your strength, then plan a strategy for getting the ball in play off the tee, even if you have to hit irons. That way you can play to your strength from the fairway.

As a general rule, get into the habit of keeping your approach shots below the hole. You'll be surprised at how much this will improve your putting. Most golfers become so focused on swing mechanics that they forget that a shot twenty feet below the hole on a sloping green is often easier than one ten feet above it.

This is especially true for chipping and pitching. On a practice day at the Scottsdale TPC with Triplett, we were investigating the most effective imagery for chips and pitches close to the green. Was it best to focus on the landing spot or to visualize the ball landing and then releasing to the hole? We decided to ask the five other PGA-TOUR players practicing that day. The consensus was that you should see the hole shot land and roll out. Your body will sense about how hard to swing and where to land the ball. Far too many players get caught up in the mechanics of the shot, or in the shot's importance to their score, and fail to concentrate on where best to leave the ball so they have the easiest possible putt. This is especially important in tournament play. Three-footers that seem easy when you are playing for fun suddenly become monsters when you have to make them under pressure. A three-foot, side-hill, downhill putt can be a beast in a tournament, so make sure you chip to a putter-friendly spot.

Putting Under Pressure

For many players, this is the part of the game where trust dissolves the quickest. They lose their 'feel' under pressure, and if visualization is taking place, it's usually negative—'seeing' the ball missing left or right or short or long. It's critical that you develop a putting pre-shot routine. It should include a trigger that activates the imaging process. I recommend taking a deep, cleansing breath just before you take the putter away. This should connect you to your imagination and help prevent negative thoughts from forming by keeping your mind in the present.

Remember, you need to allow the putter to release all the way through to the hole. Under pressure, players have a tendency either to rush the putter or to jab the putt without the proper release. According to a study of the Tour's best putters (Faxon, Crenshaw, Cink, Furyik, Riley), the time it takes to complete the full stroke is from 1.0 to 1.2 seconds and is the same whether the putt is two feet or forty.

On putts inside fifteen feet, I recommend that you 'putt by sound.' After going through your pre-shot routine, simply get the line in your imaginative mind and then stroke to the hole while maintaining a mental picture of the cup (target retention). Once your putter head has struck the ball, allow it to release toward the target. Keep your eyes focused on the spot where the ball was before you putted it, sense the release of the putter, and simply wait with your body still. Often you can see, in your mind's eye, the ball rolling true on its line toward the hole. Allow your head to release normally on your follow-through, but keep your eyes down until you actually hear the sound of the ball falling into the cup. This is 'putting by sound.' If you do this enough times, you'll come to expect that sound, and your trust in your putting will soar. Remember, because of your response to the pressure situation, tension builds, your body moves, and you may look up too soon. If you putt by sound, though, you'll get into the habit of staying still over even the most pressurized putts. This is a way to engage the imagination and to avoid thinking about the mechanics or about how important the putt may be to your score.

Patience and Posture

Besides certain horizontal, earthly pleasures, what would you rather be doing on any given day than playing golf? Why, then, do golfers tend to become impatient during a round? In a word, pressure. Pressure makes players impatient and quick in walk, talk, and swing. Patience, the antidote to pressure, comes from being at peace with yourself internally. A lack of patience can come from a preoccupation with the previous shot or from looking ahead beyond the next one. Thinking about a shot already played is, of course, a useless exercise. What can you do about it once it's over? Nothing! The shot is history.

"You should hit each shot without thinking about how to 'fix' your last one," says Laird Small, head golf professional at Pebble Beach Golf Academy in Pebble Beach, California, and 2003 National PGA Teacher of the Year. Laird and I have worked together several times, and I greatly respect his knowledge of golf. "You should have taken care of the 'fixing' in your post-shot routine," he says. "Remember, you never fix your swing during competition, but you always fix the execution of your swing. And your well-programmed S.A.T. Process is the method you use. By the time you approach your next shot, your previous shot should already be in the past in your mind. It should have no bearing on the one you are about to hit. If you can do that, it will greatly improve your game." Laird also cautions players to work on their swings during the next lesson, but never during competition.

Negative emotions like anger, frustration and fear are the real culprits when it comes to getting hung up on your past shots. They linger in the mind and are primarily created when you make judgments about your shots. "That was a terrible shot, you moron!" you hear players shout at themselves, although generally in much more colorful language. Whenever you hear that, it's time to double the bet because you can usually figure that mis-hit shot is going to stay with them a while, robbing them of the opportunity to stay in the present and hit upcoming shots with clear focus.

Don't Judge Your Shots—Describe Them!

During your practice sessions and especially during competitive rounds you should not take critical judgment with you onto the course. If you slice one into the right rough, simply shrug, say something like, "Hmmm, I hit that one to the right," and then conduct your post-shot routine. After reviewing the shot, you should replace its feel with the one you want and then walk on down the fairway. I cannot emphasize enough how important this lack of self-criticism is in terms of staying in the present and patient on the course. One way to eliminate judging your shots is to evaluate each one on your swing-tension meter. If the shot was a four, for example, give it a four and keep walking. You might say to yourself, "Well, I hung on to that one." Don't call the ball or yourself any negative names; just give the shot a four, refocus, and keep going.

Conversely, when you get something positive rolling on the course—a few birdies or pars that put you beyond what you normally shoot—the tendency is to lose patience by looking too far ahead. This is a common trap during competitive rounds when you are in or near the lead. You hear top players talk about the problem of 'getting ahead of themselves.' You've probably experienced it yourself when you had a chance to shoot a personal best or perhaps to win a tournament.

Sometimes the pressure to skip ahead in your thoughts can be even more seductive and dangerous than being angry about the shot you just hit. It isn't a negative emotion that causes the trouble in this case, but rather your own expectations.

Suspending Judgment

Your processes—pre-shot routine, post-shot routine, target retention, and tension-free swinging—help occupy your mind and keep you on track. They help you "suspend judgment," as Coach Carroll says. As you walk to your next shot, you may wish to acknowledge your own good play and the fact that you have a chance to win the tournament or shoot a personal best. Then remind yourself to stay in the present and follow the processes that you have worked so hard to establish. Gently put your expectations aside and suspend storytelling and all judgments about your swings.

Posture: El Paseo del Matador

This is one of the more overlooked aspects of peak performances. To help show yourself and others that this is your tournament and that you not only belong but fully believe you will play well, good posture is critical.

I call it "el paseo del matador," which means "the walk of the matador." Picture the matador, facing possible death, chest out, walking tall, daring the bull to charge him. That's the attitude you need to take with you onto the course. Although death is not what you will face on the course, you should stand tall and walk like a matador. What a great way to walk into every shot.

What to do Between Shots

Golf is unlike most other sports in that there is a lot of idle time between action sequences. Those who have never played the game may think that this makes it easier, but it's just the opposite. This time is to a golfer what increasing water depths are to a deep-sea diver. The deeper a diver goes, the greater the pressure. The longer the time between shots, the more the pressure on the golfer. I'm sure you know exactly what I mean. Effectively handling your time between shots is a huge challenge.

There are several ways to do this. One thing I recommend is to walk at your favorite pace and simply look at the tops of the trees around you. This keeps your posture tall and helps you aim your sights upwards. It gives you shapes and textures and colors to contemplate, and it may also give you some insight into wind direction while you are at it. Primarily, though, it is a way to activate your imaginative mind with coherent sensory information. According to Robert Ornstein, writing in *Psychology of Consciousness,* a cutting-edge publication on split-brain theory, we get access to our imaginations when we look up. We become reflective (I wonder how I stand to the cut line) as we look down. If you normally use a golf cart, get out and walk, occasionally, to restart your imagination and balance your emotions.

You may also want to talk to yourself internally. Many PGA-Touring professionals say a word or phrase over and over to themselves, which helps them focus on what they want to do. I call them 'action phrases,' and they may be something as simple as 'stay in the moment; keep in rhythm.'

Your action phrase may change from week to week, but the point is to find an auditory key that will help you stay in the present and maintain a positive mental state.

Don't feel you must stay focused strictly on golf between shots. You can think of other things as you walk, but you should avoid subjects that may put you in a negative mood and thoughts about situations over which you have no control. Think instead about how your favorite sports team is doing or perhaps a funny movie or television show you just watched. When you reach the ball, and especially as you start your pre-shot routine, you should be back into your mental 'cone of golf.'

There will be times, of course, when negative or serious thoughts from the outside world intrude. That's okay. Let them in. Acknowledge them briefly. Then tell yourself, "I can and will deal with these issues. I will do it later and I know they will be resolved. But this is not the time. Right now, I'm busy."

When you are playing a round, consider your game, at the time, the most important thing in your life. As soon as you walk off the 18th green, of course it is not.

Learn All You Can

Approach each round as a learning opportunity. If you learn something valuable during a round, you should consider your time a success, regardless of your score. Develop a course-management strategy beforehand, and then stick to it. Use all the processes you have practiced—focus on swinging tension-free; stay patient and in the present; enjoy your walks between shots; let your mind wander a bit to pleasant things; refocus at the ball by conducting your pre-shot routine, and then swing automatically, with full target retention and the freedom that trust affords. When you mis-hit a shot (Ben Hogan used to say he only hit about six shots perfectly in any given round), go through your post-shot routine, replacing that swing feel with the swing you want. Remember you should always walk 'el paseo del matador' and always resist telling the story of your round to yourself or your playing partners, even when the round is over.

During the peak season, it is not unusual for me to track scores on as many as six professional tours via the Internet. The PGA-TOUR shows us every shot, so I know the scores, often hole by hole, and other playing statistics. Still, in my phone conversations with the players I work with, whether they shot 65 or 85, I ask, "What did you learn today? How will you use what you have learned when you practice next or in tomorrow's round?" It's doubly important that this be the conversation you have with yourself as well.

Learn to recognize pressure in all its forms, including expectation, nervousness, anger, quickness, self-pity, and apathy. Have faith that your preparation and your processes will shield you from pressure. Like an umbrella in the rain, they will keep you dry while those around you, who are playing without them, are getting soaked.

16

REACHING PEAK PERFORMANCE:

Learning to Play Automatically

Everything we've covered so far in this book has been aimed at helping you reach and sustain your peak performance level. Players have a number of names for this, of course. The most common is probably 'playing in the zone.' Nearly any player on the PGA TOUR will say that you can reach this level only when the game begins to come automatically. This means that conscious thought, especially about mechanics or your score, is thrust aside, and it becomes a game, as Murphy says, "of feeling and seeing."

In psychologist-speak, playing automatically originates from a fully activated, internal-feedback system that helps guide a motor skill learned through repetition so that you are able to enter an autonomous phase dominated by kinesthetic, visual, auditory, and tactile awareness. Or, you can just say you were in the zone.

No matter how you define it, all the concepts we've talked about must be addressed if you want to play at your highest level as often as possible. Your S.A.T. Process (post-shot), self-talk, and pre-shot routine are critical to stiff-arming harmful, mechanical self-criticisms. Playing in your imaginative mind with visualization and feel opens the door to trust and to swinging freely. Paying attention to your Circle of Performance and doing things like keeping a sport journal help you develop the self-awareness necessary to move forward. Accepting confidence and deep beliefs as matters of choice, getting rid of the storytelling habit, and gaining mental toughness all help pave the way toward playing automatically. Contingency practice that prepares you for every aspect of actual competition brings it home and sets the stage for peak performances on the course.

There is no Such Thing as 'Muscle Memory'

'Muscle memory' is a misconception. It has almost become accepted wisdom that repeated practice trains our muscles so that they will know what to do. If you think about it for a moment, though, you'll realize how silly that is. Muscles have no memory at all. The central nervous system that includes the motor cortex and proprioceptors throughout the body contains the memory, but that system, however brilliant, can't swing a golf club by itself. You must engage your entire body and mind to do that. You must select a strategy—a response— and then provide the necessary stimuli to initiate the swing and allow your muscles to move freely. Your muscles must be told what to do each and every time you swing, and you must provide them with the correct data and stimuli so they will make the appropriate movement. None of this data is stored in some kind of muscle memory; it is stored in a long-term, conditioned-reflex system and has to be conjured up from scratch every time you swing.

Precise pre-shot and post-shot routines, along with the other processes we've talked about, are critical. They allow you to present similar, repetitive sets of data to your conditioned-reflex system and stimuli to your muscles for each swing. This provides consistency and trust, which in turn allow the muscles to move freely and in rhythm. Muscle memory is really about automatic, well-designed, learned processes that must be activated without conscious thought, from the central nervous system before and after each swing.

The Ideal Performance State

I've had lengthy discussions with a variety of sport psychologists, professional golfers, Coach Walsh, Coach Carroll, and a long line of knowledgeable coaches at the University of the Pacific about what defines the ideal state of athletic performance. These discussions are always exciting and they often last far into the night. Each of these experts has a unique way of defining the ideal-performance state, but I have found there are some fundamental elements upon which nearly all the great players and coaches agree. Here is a list of these elements:

> *GRACE UNDER PRESSURE*—Ernest Hemingway wrote that courage is defined as 'grace under pressure.' For golfers, courage is the ability to trigger positive emotions and actions in the face of crisis. The crisis, of course, comes in the form of a response to pressure. Pressure can stem from a fear of playing poorly or sometimes from a fear of playing too well, as in challenging a personal best score on the course or being in the hunt to win a tournament. Grace under pressure is achieved primarily and most consistently by activating the processes we've discussed, especially the pre-shot, in-between-shot, and post-shot routines, self-talk, lack of storytelling, and your choice to be self-confident.

PLAYING THE INNER GAME—This is best defined as staying focused in the present and playing with trust. Your pre-shot and post-shot routines help trigger this. A deep belief in your inner-game practice, instructors, and processes is critical. Your goals should be clear, and your expectations must be in line with the amount and quality of practice that you've been able to conduct. Take an easy walk between shots, focusing perhaps on the tops of the trees. There should be no tightness in your thoughts or your swing. Play the game for the joy it provides you at the moment. You are driven by the thought that your next swing can always be a 'ten.'

PASSION FOR EVERY MOMENT—During peak performance, your mind is calm, peaceful, and highly energized. At that moment, you are fully open, sensually speaking, to the environment around you. You are supremely confident that the processes and routines you've practiced so hard will work and that playing, now that you are on the course, will be easy. Your enjoyment of what you are doing is extremely high.

WALK OF THE MATADOR—There is nothing wrong with feeling good about yourself and your achievements. To walk like a matador does not mean being arrogant; it simply means having fun, being self-confident, and feeling good about yourself and what you can do. It means taking an appropriate pride in the work you've put into your game and in the results you've achieved. It's simply a way for you to tell the world that you are ready to meet any and all challenges because your deep belief in your game allows you to overcome all pressure and doubt.

IMAGES AND WORDS—How many times have you heard sports announcers say, "He's feeling it tonight!"? Now, how many times have you heard them say, "Wow, he's thinking about it tonight!"? Why? Because athletes don't achieve an ideal-performance state by *thinking* their way into it. They 'see' and 'feel' their way to excellence. In golf, when you are playing at the top of your game, you are most likely seeing many of the shots in your imaginative mind before you hit them. You are able to feel and perform the swing that achieves the shot you've already seen. During those shots when you don't actually see the ball flight before you swing, you probably still have a feel for what is about to happen. These kinetic elements of high performance are the most powerful when they occur in concert with affirmations, which are the positive words and action phrases you've built into your game. They come from consistent, non-judgmental, post-shot (S.A.T. Process) routines, positive self-talk, and imagery that flows automatically from shot to shot.

MENTAL TOUGHNESS—Mental toughness comes into play after hitting a shot that doesn't live up to your expectations. It isn't so much how you operate under pressure, but how you react to adversity. Mental toughness stems from your ability to establish positive deep beliefs, positive emotions, and positive self-talk, leading to a positive self-image. Your mental toughness springs from your ability to handle anger, disappointment, and frustration. How quickly can you replace negative emotions with positive ones? In an ideal-performance state, negative emotions are always short-lived.

EMOTIONAL INTELLIGENCE—Emotional intelligence
is developed through your ability to recognize and manage emotions, whether they are positive or negative, and
to control their intensity, duration, and direction. This
element is difficult to describe because the anti-con-
sciousness, anti-analytical aspect of your brain is being
exercised. It's not so much the way you coolly calculate
the distance to the pin, and dismiss the trouble left and
right, but rather how you sidestep negative emotions and
assimilate the strategic information into your imaginative
mind. Reaching peak performance almost always
involves managing your emotions and a willingness to
trust and complete immersion into the imaginative mind.

Playing Automatically!

This is the ultimate objective for athletes and golfers. Playing the
game in a seamless flow appears to require little effort or thought. In
fact, though, you achieve peak performance only when you practice
enough that your thoughts go, more or less, underground. Like a
powerful river that seems almost serene at its surface, the submerged
currents in top athletes are far more powerful than they appear. The
ultimate compliment to an athlete is that 'he makes it look easy.' In
a way, the appearance that players like Nick Watney, Annika
Sorenstam, Sam Snead, Tiger Woods, Charlie Wi, Julie Inkster, Scott
McCarron, Kirk Triplett, and others don't work hard at the game and
yet achieve marvelous results reinforces our belief that somewhere
there is a magical-swing technique that will make the game easy for
us. Don't believe it. This is a dangerous and highly destructive myth.
There are no shortcuts. These golfers worked long and hard at their
mental and physical games to get where they are. They put in thousands of hours of effort in order to make it look easy.

Peak performances are not permanent. They come and go like the tide and nobody knows exactly why. However, it should be every athlete's goal to prepare properly to reach peak performance as often as possible and stay there as long as possible. Rather than getting into the zone once every few months, you can prepare and practice so you can achieve it perhaps twice a month or more. More importantly, all the elements in this book lead to playing automatically and will allow your 'B' game to reach new heights. You may find that your 'B' game improves to such an extent that it approaches the level of your old 'A' game. When that happens, the possibilities for peak performances reach a higher level than you ever thought possible.

However, I don't want to traffic in get-rich-quick schemes here. Playing automatically takes work, practice, dedication, and patience. When you begin to practice positive self-talk, to build post-shot and pre-shot routines, and to apply all of the other lessons I've outlined in this book, you may actually experience a temporary setback in your game. Thinking about components of the mental game can squeeze out your ability to feel and see your shots. Temporarily, thinking about mental skills, like trying to trust your swing, does the same thing to your game that focusing on mechanical-swing thoughts does—it robs you of your ability to play automatically. Prepare for this and don't get frustrated if it happens the first few times you put these routines into your game. In other words, practicing self-talk during the execution of a skill can interfere with the execution of that skill until the self-talk can be done automatically. Again, don't worry about a scoring decline. It's temporary, if it happens at all. The more you conduct contingency practice, the quicker these skills will become submerged in your subconscious and allow imaginative, automatic play to emerge.

The key is to stick with it. Don't let any temporary confusion, frustration, or doubt distract you or cause you to quit. Some players experience this more intensely than others. You must believe that you are doing the right thing. You may want to customize some of these methods, concentrating on one more than another or doing one slightly differently than I've described here. We're all different. We have varying physiques and unique personalities. Don't be afraid to put your personal stamp on these procedures. Make them work for you. And make sure, in the end, that you take full responsibility for them because they must become your personal weapons if they are to work correctly.

At the same time, I am convinced, as are most of the elite players around the world, that the elements in this book—inner game, quality practice, and mental game—shine a bright light on the pathway to peak performance.

A Game of Rhythm and Tempo

One major difference between professional golfers and amateurs is that professionals consistently take all the time they need to hit a shot. By that, I don't mean they are slow. Some are, of course, but many pros also take very little time over the ball. The key word in that first sentence is 'consistently.' The top players take the same amount of time—regardless of whether they play fast or slow—for each swing. Amateurs, on the other hand, often vary the time they take from shot to shot. They might hit one shot quickly, and then stand too long over the next shot. You can almost hear the mental gears grinding as they go through their mechanical check-off lists.

The best rule of thumb for developing your own rhythm is to take all the time you need. Never hurry, but never tarry. Once you have your pre-shot routine down, you'll find that the time you take over any given shot will be remarkably similar to that of the shot you just hit and that of the one you are about to hit. You will achieve Rhythm, with a capital 'R.' Rhythm is essential to playing automatically.

John Jerome calls it 'the sweet spot in time' in his book with the same title. In his analysis, Jerome marvels at the best performers who never seem to rush, yet, at times move with incredible speed. I like the phrase 'the sweet spot in time' because it accurately describes a player who is fully engaged with the imaginative mind. As Jerome says, "When an athlete is hitting the internal sweets spots, when the timing is right, the motion is remarkably smooth."

Deep Beliefs

To play automatically, your deep beliefs must be in order. You must believe in yourself, and that comes from having full confidence in your technique, mental game, practice, and instruction. Although you may not have a world-class swing, remember that the swing you have today is the one you will play with today. So, use it and trust it. Don't change your technique in the middle of a competitive round or during warm-up. Instead, use the tools you have, and concentrate on the inner-game skills you've developed.

Zen and Ten

I am always intrigued by the parallels I see between some of the concepts of applied sport psychology and those of Zen Buddhism. Los Angeles Lakers coach Phil Jackson is famous for using Zen concepts to motivate his Lakers and Chicago Bulls teams, and even Shaq and Kobe bought into them. Too bad there wasn't more in Phil's Zen repertoire about them getting along with each other, but the point is, there is plenty of room in sports for the practice of Zen beliefs.

Perhaps golfers use them more than other athletes. McCarron has been an advocate of Zen practices for some time, and we often comment that Buddha would have been a low handicapper. For example, Zen teachings say that the third, and lowest, stage of consciousness is borrowed consciousness. Astute followers of Zen may accuse me of oversimplification, but as the name implies, this is what I call the storytelling state of consciousness. It's a created consciousness that does not necessarily jibe with reality. Much of it is fictional, created to appease the wounded pride and deflated ego of the storyteller. It takes golfers far away from an ideal-performance state and implies a lack of responsibility, accountability, and truthfulness.

The second stage of consciousness is also not ideal for athletes. This is forward or backward thinking, and for golfers, it means thinking about the next hole or the shot just hit. Players project themselves ahead or get caught in the eddy of their past shots. Obviously, peak performances don't often arise out of this second stage.

The first, and highest, stage of consciousness is what one should strive for on and off the golf course. It means being 100 percent present in the here and now. That includes time in-between-shots, as well. For golfers, it means focusing totally on the shot at hand, engaging the imaginative mind, seeing the ball flight, and feeling the swing. This first stage is where great performances are born. It is where the sweet spot in time exists.

A key concept that will allow you to stay in this highest stage of consciousness for the longest period of time is the understanding that the perfect swing is the one you trust. A ten is a swing with no tension, but it is liberating to know that you don't need tens to play fantastic golf. Depending on how you evaluate your swings, an average of sevens throughout your round should get you to par, or at least allow you to challenge your personal best. An average of eights or nines will almost assuredly provide you with a personal best and allow you to win most of the competitions you enter. You don't need tens to win. You don't even need a nine average to reach your peak performance. You just need to be firmly entrenched in the present, trust your swing, and play automatically.

17

IN THE WINNER'S CIRCLE

The chances are great that at some point in your golf career you've experienced what it takes to enter the winner's circle. Whether it's the Masters, the U.S. Open, a mini-tour stop, an amateur championship, your club championship, the fourth flight of your club championship, or a two-dollar Nassau with friends, there is nothing quite like winning. It is a culmination of effort, proper practice, adherence to *Winning-the-Battle-Within* processes, and ultimately, a swing that you trust. There is usually a good dose of courage and resolve thrown in as well.

Let's face it. Winning is fun and can yield great rewards. Yet, golf is a game with many participants and only one winner. Nobody wins all the time. That's why it is important to understand and embrace the fact that playing well is its own special reward. Regardless of your position on the scoreboard, if you prepare properly, trust your swing, play your inner game, practice positive self-talk, utilize your pre-shot, in-between-shot, and post-shot routines, and take the other critical steps we've discussed, you should feel proud of yourself and your round. As you reach a deeper understanding of the game, you'll realize that the sensory and emotional internal feedback you give yourself can count for more than the external feedback you receive from others.

Yet there is no denying that winning can generate strong emotions, especially if your victory is the result of a classic, head-to-head dual that comes down to the last putt, with everything on the line. This is the moment we all dream about and, more importantly, for which we should prepare every time we set foot on a practice tee or green.

Bill Walsh on Winning

Bill knew what it took to get to the winner's circle, having built the 49ers into the most successful football team of its era. I remember a skiing trip Bill and I took shortly after the 49ers won the 1989 Super Bowl in dramatic fashion over the stubborn Cincinnati Bengals. As we were riding a long ski lift to the top of a mountain, we talked about the famous last drive, led by quarterback Joe Montana, that lifted the 49ers to victory. The 49ers were trailing 16 to 13 with a little more than three minutes left in the game. The 49ers had the ball, and it was first and ten, but they were 92 yards from their end zone.

"We could have stepped back and thrown three long passes to Jerry Rice and said we were trying to win the game," Bill told me. "Most fans would have accepted that, but we had spent years preparing for that moment. Nobody panicked. We had simulated this type of situation hundreds of times in practice. We ran a number of plays, mixing in a little bit of everything, running, passing, and just doing all the things we knew how to do. When we finally scored and won the game, I don't think anybody on our team was surprised. We just did the things we had practiced. Winning isn't any more complicated than that."

Bill also summed up the approach that Montana and the other players took during those pressurized moments. "Our people were calm and intense," he said.

I've always liked that description—'calm and intense.' It comes as close to describing what a golfer's mental state should be during competition as any phrase I've ever heard. It's important to point out that intensity does not mean tension. In fact, playing with calm intensity is the antithesis of playing with tension. It describes a mental state that gives a golfer the best possible chance to be successful. Because you know you can perform automatically, calm intensity means your senses are wide open, your imagination is fully activated, and your confidence is locked in.

Does this mean that if you are calm and intense and your practice has been faithful you are assured of entering the winner's circle in every tournament? Of course not. Jack Nicklaus finished second more than any other player in the history of the PGA TOUR. What that indicates is Nicklaus put himself in a position to succeed more than any other player. Winning is not something we can make happen every time we tee it up. Too many unpredictable factors, including a lucky or unlucky bounce now and then or great play by a competitor, are involved to be able to control them all. But, getting to the winner's circle is no accident. Those who win the most often are those who are better prepared. You can't win every tournament or match, but you can prepare to give yourself the best chance to compete at a high level. That's why I like the saying that "Winning isn't everything, but preparing and playing to win are."

McCarron's First Win

Most of us remember our first big win in golf, and Scott is no exception. "It took me some time to mature in golf, to realize that preparing for a round is like a CEO of a company preparing for a meeting," Scott recalled. "You really must have all of your ducks in a row. I used to think that only meant having a well-tuned swing. Working with the concepts embedded in *Winning the Battle Within* helped me realize how limited that approach is. We'd go through a checklist of things before the start of a tournament and before and after each round. In retrospect, I realize how well prepared I was before the start of the Freeport-McDermott Classic in New Orleans some time ago.

"I was feeling positive going into the tournament for several reasons. I had just helped Glen with a two-day, mental-training seminar. I'd worked with Glen before at seminars, but this time I concentrated fully on everything that was being said, and I picked up a lot of positive energy. By the end of the workshop, I was anxious to hit some balls at the range and practice some of the concepts we had talked about. It was dark, but Glen and I went out to the range anyway. The moon was full and illuminated the hitting area for us, creating a magical launching pad to a moon-target. That was an incredibly powerful experience.

"I had played well at the end of the previous year, and I felt myself intentionally re-creating that mindset. I was free of swing thoughts. I was connected to the targets mentally, and when I was ready to swing, I kept a strong visual picture of the target in my mind's eye—from takeaway to impact. I worked patiently through all my mental processes. That gave me a feeling that I can only describe as one of freedom. It raised the level of my confidence in all areas.

"Before the tournament, I bought some motivational cards with scenic golf photographs and inspirational messages on them. The first card focused on opportunity, the second was about passion, and the third dealt with perseverance. I read over the messages each night of the tournament as I prepared for the next round.

"During the tournament, I was relaxed but focused on the processes we had worked on—pre-shot routines, great self-talk, solid course management, a trusting swing, and great posture. I constantly reminded myself to feel that this was my tournament and that I was the host. The sum of all these parts was that I was able to play automatically when it most counted. As the pressure grew toward the end of the fourth day, I had complete trust in the inner-game processes I had built and in my swing. I wasn't bothered by swing thoughts; I just let it go. A tremendous thrill runs through you when as it all comes together like that. You're relaxed, but it's exciting at the same time. I was having so much fun that I wasn't ready to stop playing when I walked off the 72nd hole. I felt that was reward enough, but the next day I received the winner's check. That was fun, too."

Scott has won twice since his New Orleans triumph, both times at the Bell-South Championship, and I fully expect him to add more victories before long.

Kirk Triplett's Journey to the Winner's Circle

"Early in the year 2000, I was taking a lot of heat about being the leading money winner on the PGA TOUR who hadn't yet won a tournament," Kirk recalls. "I was letting it bother me, until Glen and I talked it over, and we agreed that it was pretty damn good to be the leading money winner on the PGA TOUR who hadn't yet won. We went to work on the methods that Glen introduced to me, and I began to play with more confidence and less conscious thought.

"In 2000, I played the Los Angeles Open at Riviera Country Club, where I had met with mixed success in the past. I had always been somewhat tough on myself—I guess you could say my self-talk wasn't as task specific and supportive as it should have been—

and I focused on changing that during the week. I played well and found myself in contention on the final day. Tiger Woods and David Duval were close to the lead, and I expected somebody to make a move. I made birdies on the seventh and ninth holes, and when I looked up at the turn, I realized that the guy making the move was me! I took the lead, and the pressure grew. I made a few mistakes, but instead of getting down on myself like I'd had a tendency to do in the past, I kept reminding myself that even the guy who wins the tournament makes some mistakes along the way. It was a hard thing for me to do after all those years of being judgmental, but I accepted the challenge. I didn't get ahead of myself, and my internal talk was positive. I just said, 'I have the lead, but I've prepared for it during practice. Let's just play the back nine and see what happens.'

"From there on, it all came down to staying patient and hitting the shot in front of me. I took responsibility for every shot and every decision and never gave a thought to telling stories.

"By the time we reached the 18th green, Woods and Duval had fallen back, and I was battling it out with Jesper Parnevik, my playing partner. He had a 30-foot putt for birdie, and I had a tough little downhill four-footer for par. I was two strokes ahead, so he had to make his putt to force me to make mine. Just before he hit his putt, I caught myself thinking he wasn't going to make it. I knew right then that I had to get more positive. I accepted the probability that he would make it, and I got into the mindset that I was going to make mine. I wasn't consciously doing self-talk; it all happened quickly. I was very quiet in my mind. Jesper did make his putt, but because I was prepared, it didn't shake me. I was totally focused on going through my putting routine properly. I trusted it, let it go automatically, and the ball dropped dead center.

"In retrospect, I feel I won that tournament because I did a good job of not beating myself up when I mis-hit shots. No matter

where I found myself on the golf course, I remained focused solely on the next shot. I felt, and I still feel, that if we golfers can master Glen's lessons, we can play like the great ones play—one shot
at a time."

A Matter of Excellence

A concept that I've always associated with the winner's circle is
excellence. Entering the winner's circle requires a combination of
physical and mental excellence from a golfer. Excellence is a concept *and* a goal. Achieving it is a journey *and* a destination. It's
easy to understand excellence as a destination. Like winning,
excellence is something we strive for—a goal to be reached on
treasured occasions. To me, though, the first part of the statement
is the most riveting. Understanding the pursuit of excellence as a
journey is what gives golf its texture and makes it one of the most
challenging games ever invented. It is also the concept that makes
golf equal parts ecstasy and agony. It is what addicts us to the
game. It is the powerful attraction that brings us back to play again
and again. After all, in golf, your next swing can always be a ten.

The journey toward excellence, which is the pathway to the
winner's circle, is littered with challenges. Each game is a journey
in itself, filled with potential triumph and heartbreak. Each shot is
a two-edged sword, with excellence on one edge and disaster on the
other. The achievement of excellence is elusive, but we are all
inspired by the knowledge that on any given day, on any given shot,
it is indeed within our grasp.

Why Winning is Difficult

What makes golf such a game of the heart is that your performance
is open to public scrutiny. Others can easily judge you according to

the scores you post and how well you perform. The better the performance, the sharper the lens of judgment. Judgment and expectations set by others make it difficult to enter the winner's circle on
a consistent basis. Not only must you follow the precipitous pathway of excellence toward the top of the mountain, but the higher
you climb, the more judgment befalls you. That irony can be seen
in the sports' headlines of the newspapers. If a PGA player, for
example, takes a lead into the final round of the Masters and plays
well on the fourth day, but still loses by one stroke, it's likely the
headlines will state that the player 'lost' the Masters. This is unin-
formed and ridiculous, of course. If you finish second in the
Masters, you haven't lost anything. Finishing second is, in itself, a
magnificent feat. But, who said that life or the media were fair?
That's why it's critical to acknowledge that while you may not be
able to control the judgment that comes from public scrutiny, you
can control how it affects you internally. You can learn to minimize
its importance and to refrain from judging yourself.

The price of failing to do these things is high. Succumbing to
external pressures—by allowing them to become internal—can
lead even strong players to doubt themselves and to consider themselves losers when indeed they are not. If you want to enjoy the
game and to continue to improve as a player, you must not allow
self-judgment to mount. A great example of a player who is able to
do this is Tom Watson. Watson, as you may remember, faded in the
stretch several times early in his career. Had he listened to the
whispers and believed the headlines, he might have quit believing
in himself. But, he didn't. He focused on the pursuit of excellence
and believed in his journey and in the correctness of his path. Over
time, he learned how to win, and ultimately, he became one of the
great champions of all time.

Evaluating Your Journey Toward Excellence

Defining your own journey toward excellence with task specific and supportive self-talk helps create positive deep beliefs that are a distinctive feature of progressive improvement. Part of your improvement depends on objectively evaluating your efforts as you go. Whenever your game breaks down, you are presented with a wonderful opportunity to employ nonjudgmental evaluations, reassert your deep beliefs, reinstate positive self-talk, check your practice regimens, and continue your journey.

Below are some pitfalls that you must learn to avoid as you climb the path to excellence. Remember, don't beat yourself up when you encounter them and fall prey to their insidious interference. Be objective. Evaluate, replace, and move on. Performance breakdowns may be caused when a golfer:

- Loses trust due to focusing on outcome rather than on process
- Loses concentration due to a lack of patience caused by looking ahead to the next shot or failing to move past mis-hit shots;
- Makes consistent mistakes involving the S.A.T. Process;
- Is too pumped up (intensity becomes tension);
- Lacks trust in execution due to improper practice;
- Lacks trust in his instruction or instructor;
- Has not learned the necessary mental and inner-game skills;
- Lacks motivation;
- Forces the action or movement;
- Lacks commitment;
- Mismanages emotions;

- Suffers from injury or fatigue, or
- Lacks attentiveness to the task at hand.

All of these symptoms are temporary. They can be serious distractions if given any attention. If you evaluate them objectively and replace them with the mental and inner-game skills you've honed with quality practice you will see progressive improvement.

Winning the Battle Within

There is glory and joy in the game of golf, as well as agony and angst. Certainly, some of you will continue to pursue the perfect technical swing, but I hope I have succeeded in convincing most of you that another journey awaits you that is far more rewarding—the journey toward finding your own inner strengths. Real glory and deep joy lies in discovering and developing those strengths.

There is virtually no limit to your improvement as a golfer when you make learning to trust your swing your primary goal. Because there are as many 'perfect swings' as there are successful golfers, trust is the key concept. You will be surprised at how effective your swing will become, no matter how unorthodox it appears to be, if you decide to trust it. Trust can be elusive, and many golfers, particularly those who seek improvement solely in the latest swing fixes and equipment offerings, fail to find it. But, lasting trust is not something you find or buy—it is something you develop within yourself. The keys to the development of trust are the inner-game and mental skills that are learned through quality practice.

They include the S.A.T. Process and the understanding and acceptance of the importance of playing in the imaginative mind. They also include paying attention to your performance profile and keeping a sport journal where many clues, self-discoveries, and lessons can be captured for later use. Trust is also formed by ending storytelling, welcoming others to 'your' tournament, maintaining good posture, developing mental toughness, creating positive self-imagery, and imitating *el paseo del matador!* The foundation of trust is laid through the proper repetition of quality contingency and inner-game practice routines and through executing the skills developed through them on the golf course. Along the way, critical elements, like your pre-shot routine and consistent, positive self-talk are locked into the harmony of your swing and your game.

Even if you've secretly doubted yourself and your game for years, you can change those old tapes and build deep beliefs. You can choose to be confident. You can become an intuitive, imaginative, creative player and give yourself the best possible chance to compete every time out. Your golfing identity is not set in stone. You can learn to do old things in new ways. All of us can learn to play, as Coach Walsh said, with "calm intensity." All of us can learn to play with trust, freedom, and the improvisational joy of Thelonious Monk. All of us can find the harmony, grace, and glory that the game of golf so generously offers, if we remember that the perfect swing is the one we trust. It is then that we give ourselves the best possible chance to win the battle within.

APPENDIX

QUESTIONNAIRES

GOLF SELF-IMPROVEMENT QUESTIONNAIRE
(adapted from Terry Orlick, Pursuit of Excellence, 1990.)

Used at the start of workshops and consultations.

These questions are designed to help you reflect upon your personal golf history and to help you develop or refine a pre-competition plan and a competition focus plan.

Knowing your competition self:

1. Think of your all-time best golf performance(s) and respond to the following questions keeping that event(s) in mind:

How did you feel just before starting play?

No activation   0 1 2 3 4 5 6 7 8 9 10   Highly activated
    (mentally and   (mentally and
    physically flat)   physically charged)

Not worried   0 1 2 3 4 5 6 7 8 9 10   Extremely worried
or scared at all   or scared

2. What were you saying to yourself or thinking shortly before the start of the round or tournament?

3. How were you focused during the round; i.e., what were you aware of or paying attention to while actively engaged in the performance?

4.   Now think of your worst competitive round or tournament performance(s) and respond to the following questions keeping that game in mind:

How did you feel just before that round or tournament?

No activation   0 1 2 3 4 5 6 7 8 9 10   Highly activated
   (mentally and   (mentally and
   physically flat)   physically charged)

Not worried   0 1 2 3 4 5 6 7 8 9 10   Extremely worried
or scared at all   or scared

5.   What were you saying to yourself or thinking shortly before the start of that round or tournament?

6.   How were you focused during the round or tournament (i.e., what were you aware of or paying attention to while actively engaged in the performance)?

7.   What were the major differences between your thinking (or feelings) prior to these two performances (i.e., best an worst)?

8.   What were the major differences in your focus of attention during these (i.e., best and not-so best)?

9.   How would you prefer to feel just before an important round or tournament?

No activation   0 1 2 3 4 5 6 7 8 9 10   Highly activated
   (mentally and   (mentally and
   physically flat)   physically charged)

10.   How would you prefer to focus your attention during an important performance?

11.   Is there anything you would like to change about the way you approach a competition or practice?

12.   Is there anything you would like your coach or instructor to change in the way they instruct you?

IMAGINATION & AWARENESS QUESTIONNAIRE

Designed to evaluate your imagination and awareness of your internal feed-back system

In each category rate your awareness on a 1-10 scale (1 being low to 10 being high). The first column is for your current rating and the second column rating is determined after a systematic practice of inner game drills.

1. Do you consistently use a planned
    pre-shot procedure?   ____   ____
2. Do you have a golf grip you trust?   ____   ____
3. Are your aware of consistently setting up
    in a fundamentally solid address position
    before each swing?   ____   ____
4. Are you aware of aligning your body
    before you swing?   ____   ____
5. Are you aware of walking into your final
    address position in the same way for every
    shot or stroke?   ____   ____
6. Are you aware of the tempo of your take-away?   ____   ____
7. Are you aware of a transition at the top of
    your back swing?   ____   ____
8. Are you aware of releasing or not releasing
    through the ball at the target?   ____   ____
9. Are you aware of your swing tempo?   ____   ____
10. Are you aware of the rhythm and balance
    of your swing?   ____   ____
11. Are you aware of how you look when
    you swing?   ____   ____
12. Are you aware, of how your swing feels for
    best performance?   ____   ____
13. Can you generate these feelings consistently?   ____   ____
14. Do you trust your swing, particularly
    under pressure?   ____   ____

15. Are you aware of retaining the image of your
    target or ball flight throughout your swing?   _____   _____
16. Are you aware of visualizing the flight of
    the ball anytime before you swing?   _____   _____
17. Are you aware of feeling the swing that
    matches what you see?   _____   _____

EMOTIONAL INTELLIGENCE QUESTIONNAIRE

This questionnaire was developed from the discussion of Three Minds in
Emotional Intelligence, by Daniel Goleman.

1. What is the most frequent method you use to activate your conscious
    mind in practice and performance for golf?
2. How do you most frequently activate your imaginative mind during
    practice and performance for golf?
3. What part of your imagination do you most frequently activate during
    practice and performance? (kinesthetic feel, visualization, hearing, touch)
4. What are the most frequent positive emotions you experience during the
    practice and performance of golf? (joy, excitement, calmness, passion,
    appreciation)
5. What situations typically cause you to activate these emotions?
6. What methods do you use to maintain these positive emotions?
7. What are the most frequent negative emotions you experience during the
    practice and performance of golf? (anger, fear, anxiety, sadness, frustra-
    tion, apathy)
8. What situations typically cause you to activate these emotions?
9. What methods do you use during practice and play, to control the nega-
    tive emotions?

        a. the intensity of the emotions?

        b. the direction of the emotions?

        c. the duration of the emotions?

WINNING THE BATTLE WITHIN CHECK LIST

Name _____

Date _____

On a scale of 1 (low) –10 (high) graduated scale, rate your progress within each category. Use the checklist at the start of each week, before a string of tournaments, or as you approach important events. Use the same sheet the following week and compare your evaluations. Make your own copies.

	Current Rating	*Comments*

Self-confidence (internal) _____

Self-talk (task specific &

supportive)_____

Imagery (see, feel, touch, hear)_____

Posture _____

Attitude _____

Motivation (internal & external) _____

Managing emotions

(See HeartMath.com or wbwgolf.com for explanations)

    Consistency of heart

    lock-in practice _____

    Getting to neutral _____

    Quick coherence

    (practice and play)_____

Pre-shot routine

(commitment to strategy) _____

Pre-shot routine Aiming

(club, mind, body)_____

Pre-shot routine

(trusting my swing) _____

	Current Rating	*Comments*

Tension free swings (rhythm,
tempo, in sync) _____

Trusting my swing under pressure _____

Communication with caddie _____

Course strategy
(commitment & execution) _____

Quality practice (intensity,
concentration, content) _____

Simulated practice (random &
variable)_____

Technique practice (blocked) _____

Inner game practice (five in a row,
eyes closed, low energy, tension
free, breath) _____

Tournament site practice
(consistency of regimen) _____

Competition day warm-up_____

Fitness maintenance _____

Nutrition and health _____

Recovery (emotional & physical) _____

Personal relationships _____

Post-shot routine (anchoring,
refocusing, suspending judgment) _____

Organizational (business or school) _____

Contact with coaches _____

Equipment _____

Goal setting (short and long term) _____

Sticking to action plans_____

Evaluation (stats, schedule,
goals, practice, performance) _____

Relative to your current self-ratings, which categories receive your highest ratings - strengths you would like to maximize? Also, which performance categories would you like to give immediate attention? Select two to three performance categories and outline how, when and where you will maintain or improve your self-rating, (this week, this series of tournaments, practice, etc.)

Category_____

_____

Category_____

_____

Category_____

_____

PRACTICE DRILLS

Create a shot challenge (9 ball challenge)

Learn to use the TENSION FREE, TRUST routine. Hit each shot executing your pre-shot routine. Use your post-shot routine following unsatisfactory shots. NO REPEATS!

Warm up hitting 10 shots to a target developing a feel for a *tension free swing*. Use a pitching wedge.

Using 8, 7, 6, and 5 irons, hit each shot listed below in any combination you choose. Hit all shots with one club, and then move to your next club. *There are no repeat swings allowed.* A right-to-left shot must be followed by a left-to-right or straight shot.

- Straight, low, and normal high, (trajectories),
- Fade, slice, hook, or draw.
- Left-to-right or right-to-left shots should never cross over the flag or target.

Interval yardage: distance control

Learn to develop an internal distance control yardage clock for your wedges. At your range set out soccer cones from 50 to 120 yards, at 10-yard intervals. At first, use blocked practice – numerous repetitions at each distance - to lock in distances control for each interval. Use all of your wedges and your 8 and 9 irons.

After you have developed distance control, randomize practice by aiming for a different distance on each shot and use your pre and post-shot routines.

Creativity

These drills promote creativity of seeing and feeling. Note that you should incorporate pre and post shot routines into these drills.

1. Call Your Shot. This drill is fun to play with a partner. You may call the shot, or your partner may call your shot.
2. Play the Course. You may visualize your favorite course, or the course you are preparing to play in a qualifying or tournament round. Time will dictate how many holes you choose to play. Hit every shot on a given hole until your ball is on the green. Then move to the next tee.
3. Extended Rope: Place the rope on your target line starting 20 yards in front of the ball. In your address position, look down the rope on the target line and target. As your eyes move back to the ball retain the image of the rope that is extended to the target. Also, complete the same drill with your eyes closed at impact. Swing down the imagined target line.

Alignment

Walk into your address position with the alignment of your choice; use parallel left as a reference point with your bodyline pointing at a target approximately 2-3 yards to left of, and parallel to your target line. Use an intermediate spot in front of the ball (no more then 12") in line to the target in order to line up your clubface. Use a coach to check your alignment or face into a full-length mirror and check yourself. Repeat the drill 20 times without swinging the club. Change targets!

ADDITIONAL SHORT GAME DRILLS (adapted from David Cook)

Note that you can do several of the other drills (i.e., eyes closed, look at the target) and each of these short game drills simultaneously.

Around the World (putting). In a circle, place eight tees at 4' around a hole. Distance can change according to your needs. You should now have eight spots (tees) from which to putt at the hole. Using your full routine, make the 4-footers. You must putt your last 4-footer with your eyes closed. You are allowed two opportunities to make each putt. If you miss twice, you must begin again. You can make this game more difficult by giving yourself only one opportunity to make each putt. Keep score by keeping your total number of putts.

Ladder drill (putting). Find a slight to moderate slope on your practice green. Place five; 4-foot long strings approximately 18-24 inches apart. The strings should be placed parallel to one another so that they resemble a ladder. Place a tee six-feet from each of the end-strings. Using one ball, the object is to putt the ball into each 18-24 inch space in sequence. Since there are five strings, there are four spaces. Putt at the space nearest you, which is space 1, until the ball stops in that space. Then putt to spaces 2, 3, 4, 3, 2, and 1. Once again, you must putt to the designated space until the ball stops in that space. Keep score by keeping your total number of putts.

Five-string distance drill (putting, chipping, lob, shots, bunker shots). Place a string at one end of the practice green. Step off 20, 30, 40, 50, and 60 feet, placing a string at each of these distances. These strings should be parallel to the string you will putt from at the other end of the green. Using five balls, putt one ball to each string. Keep score by measuring (if you don't have a tape measure in your bag, you may approximate) your total distance for the five balls.

3 x 3 drill (chipping, lob shots, bunker shots). Place three strings on the green, equidistant apart. You may determine the length of the shots desired. Hit three balls with three different clubs, from three different lies to the first target. Then repeat the process to the second and third targets. Use your creativity to change distance, shot variety, and targets.

INNER GAME DRILLS

Through the inner game drills you'll learn to trust your swing, play more fully in your imaginative mind, and swing automatically. You will feel your inner game strengthening almost immediately. The inner-game drills include methods to improve tempo, rhythm, and the synchronization of your swing. During all drills use your abbreviated pre-shot routine

The Tension-free Drill

The tension-free drill is best done with a partner, but you can easily do it on your own. After each shot, the golfer hitting the ball tells his 'coaching' partner, how much tension he felt in his swing. The 'hitter' should rate his or her shots by choosing a number from a scale of 1-10, with the number one indicating a tension-filled swing and the number ten, a tension-free swing.

Low Energy and Full Release

Take a club – let's say a five iron – and aim at a target that is about 75 percent of your normal five-iron distance. Take a full swing, making sure you finish the swing completely. It should appear as though you have just made a full swing in slow motion.

The drill is designed to allow the player to experiment with gauging the correct rhythm and tempo that allows the swing to come in on the beat and keep the ball on line.

You can use any club in the drill. Most players find the drill very effective while using a driver.

Eyes Closed at Impact

Take your stance with your eyes open. Begin your swing. Just before your club gets to impact close your eyes. By shutting your eyes only at impact, it still forces you to trust your swing, and you'll get clearer and more precise internal feedback about how the club head feels as it passes through the impact zone.

Target Retention and the Imaginative Eye

Throughout the swing – from the takeaway to the top of the backswing and down through the impact zone — the image of your ball landing on an exact spot should remain foremost in your imaginative mind. This method of target-focus practice is an initial step toward inclusion of target retention in your pre-shot routine and during your swing.

Let it Go!

Arrange five balls in a row so you can hit them in quick succession. The idea is to hit one shot, then immediately set up and hit the next one. You should come to a stop and address each shot before taking the next swing. Because the swings are in rapid succession, there is little time to judge your previous shot or to allow conscious-swing thoughts to intrude. It's great fun with a driver, although it usually works well with any club.

Breathe and Swing!

Assume your address position with your abbreviated routine, and as you take your last look at the target, inhale and then exhale as your eyes come back to the ball. Then swing! The breath does two things: it brings you back to the present and relieves stress. Make sure the breath inhale/exhale takes about 6 seconds. Make sure your diaphragm expands and the breath comes from your belly. Experiment with the timing of the breath and eventually it will become automatic.

DEVELOPING A PRE-SHOT ROUTINE (chapter eleven)

WHAT IS YOUR S.A.T. SCORE?

Strategy: Survey the area and make a commitment. Strategy must fit the moment, the situation and your skill:

- Target selection: Choose your aiming spot and target.
- Shot selection: Total commitment.
- Club selection: Conservative strategy equals a confident swing.
- See and feel the shape of the shot.

Trigger: To move away from your conscious, thinking mind in order to give your imagination the freedom to act.

Aiming:

- Aim your clubface to the target and/or an intermediate spot.
- Align your body to the target and shape of the shot.
- Aim your mind to the target.
- See the target: Visualize your shot.
- Feel the swing.
- Use action phrases to connect with the swing.

Trust:

- Let go of conscious control.
- Allow your swing to find the path of least resistance.
- Trust what you see and feel.

Breathe:

- Place a breath in your routine.
- Either as a trigger to move from your conscious mind to your imagination, or just before you swing, or both times.
- It helps a player become present and relieves tension.

ACTION PHRASES

- Single words or short phrases that connect your imagination to para-graphs of movement. Typically, phrases emerge from your best performance profiles. What do you say, feel and see when you are playing your best game? Action phrases relate to tempo, rhythm, and whole swing movements.
- Words connect to visualization (pictures) to kinesthetic awareness (body movement feelings). They link what we feel and see. When we are swinging at our best we generate the most effective action phrases.
- Elite players develop a library of words and phrases that join with the grace, power and flow of a synchronized golf swing.
- Action phrases can be used at any time during a concentration routine: from behind the ball, on the walk to the address position, during alignment procedures, prior to swinging and while swinging. They are specific to each situation, player and the skill to be executed.

- Action phrases are not to be confused with conscious swing thoughts or keys for swing mechanics.
- Action phrase examples: Choose from the list or create your own.

Tempo • Release • Rhythm • Free it up • Aim • Go • See
Turn and go • Target • Aggressive • Feel • Down the line
Trust • Line up • Smooth • Swing

DEVELOPING A POST-SHOT ROUTINE-S.A.T. PROCESS

Great Shots: When you hit your best shots pose and allow the feeling of your swing and the positive emotion to deeply embed in your long-term memory.

Missed Shots:
- When mistakes happen: mental toughness begins.
- Suspend judgment.
- Missed shots are caused by a breakdown in execution.
- Begin the review, replace, & refocus process by describing your shot non-judgmentally, verbally and non-verbally.

STRATEGY:
- Were you committed?
- Did the strategy fit your skill and the situation?

AIMING:
- How were your bodylines?
- Ball Position?
- Weight Distribution?
- Imagination to the target?

TRUST:
Awareness is the key to trust, sensing miscalculations in rhythm, tempo, synchronization, tension-free, and letting go.

REVIEW – REPLACE – REFOCUS.

THE PERFORMANCE PACKAGE

Five Performance Routines (adapted from Neale Smith)

- A set routine for how you will play the course.
- Set your pre-shot routine. Your SAT is reviewed and practiced – ready for all situations.
- Set your post-shot routine. Love the great ones allowing the swing feel to flow deeply into your body/mind. After miss-hits, suspend judgment, and re-focus for the next shot within 30 seconds max.
- Set your between-shots routine. Always walk tall – el paseo del matador – head up to the tops of trees, clouds or space. Engage in conversation if appropriate. Anything to stay in the present.
- A post-round routine. You might lose the game (round), but you'll never lose the lesson. What can I take forward to my next practice session or play?

GOLF PRACTICE AND PERFORMANCE GOALS: *SHORT FORM*

Complete the following:
- Dream Goals
- Task-specific goals
- Action Plans

GOALS: (Begin by stating your dream goals)
- What is your long-term dream goal in golf? What is potentially possible in the long term if you stretch your limits?
- What is your dream goal for golf performance this year? What is potentially possible if all your limits are stretched the year?
- What do you feel is a realistic performance goal that you can achieve this year, based on your present skill level, on your potential for improvement and on your current motivation?

Note that there are two types of goals you are asked to determine for yourself. The first are dream goals. These are general outcome/result oriented goals. You may set some short term and long term goals in this area such as a top-10 finish in a tournament, making the Americas Cup team, making the All-AJGA, making a college team, being on the PGA Tour, or winning the fourth flight of your club championship.

These dream goals can motivate, help give you a sense of mission, and lead you over time. They are the passions that fuel your engine.

The second type is task goals. Task goals refer to the actions performed to develop a specific skill within a category in the circle of performance. The specific skill's accomplishment is one of the tasks to becoming a great golfer. Task goals should be something over which you have control. Task goals are divided into seven categories.

Examples under each category could be:

1. Improved golf mechanics (i.e., driving, chipping, putting, club head speed)
2. Physical conditioning goals (i.e., strength, flexibility, endurance)
3. Inner game goals (i.e., trusting your swing, tension control, having fun)
4. Mental skill goals (i.e., self-confidence, self-talk, emotional management, pre, post and in between shot routines)
5. Organizational goals (i.e., tournament preparation, tournament logistics, equipment selection, training session planning, communication with instructors or sports organization)
6. Personal goals (i.e., things you do with free time, personal relationships, education, work, recreation, recovery)
7. Practice goals (i.e., learning new skills, simulated practice, pre competition, inner game)

Under each task goal listed, you are asked to specify the method that will assist you to achieve your goals. For example, a golf performance goal may be to improve your sand shot technique. A method of achieving this goal could be specific changes in mechanics, practice time in a variety of conditions, or using a tracking technique with video coverage by an instructor or friend. In setting your goals, pick areas you have already perfected and want to improve as well as areas you may be weak at and need to learn something new. Remember, goals change over time. Be flexible and when appropriate, change your goals.

It is important that each day in your task goal you have an activity that provides excitement and fun.

III. Action Plans

Now that you have identified task goals, develop an action plan to achieve these goals. It won't be possible to focus on all of your goals at one time. Select two or three goals from different groups that you can devote significant time toward achieving in the next three weeks. Select additional goals you can devote concentrated energy toward over the following three to six week period. For the group of goals you will begin working on, include a specific schedule of activities and follow through. You may have to revise your plan as things unfold, but start with a plan and you will achieve great results.

First Segment Plan:

Goal #1: _____
Activity Schedule _____
_____

Goal #2: _____
Activity Schedule _____
_____

Goal #3: _____
Activity Schedule _____
_____

Goal #4: _____
Activity Schedule _____
_____

Goal #5: _____
Activity Schedule _____
_____

Goal #6: _____
Activity Schedule _____
_____